CHURCH, COMMUNITY, AND STATE

Volume I

THE CHURCH AND ITS FUNCTION
IN SOCIETY

THE CHURCH AND ITS FUNCTION IN SOCIETY

by

W. A. VISSER 'T HOOFT

AND

J. H. OLDHAM

LONDON
GEORGE ALLEN & UNWIN LTD
MUSEUM STREET

FIRST PUBLISHED IN 1937

CONTENTS

CONTENTS

PREFACE

This volume has been written in connection with the Conference at Oxford on Church, Community, and State. It is plain that the relation of the Church to the Community and to the State can be profitably considered only in the light of two fundamental questions. The first is the nature of the Church. The second is the functions of the Church in relation to society. These two questions are the subject of the present volume. Dr. W. A. Visser 't Hooft deals with the first in Chapters I to III, and the rest of the volume is concerned with the second.

Six other volumes in connection with the Oxford Conference are in preparation and will be published, it is hoped, in the autumn of the present year. Several references to them are made in the following pages. Each of these volumes contains contributions from writers in different countries representing different Christian traditions. The titles of the volumes are:

> *The Christian Understanding of Man.*
> *The Kingdom of God and History.*
> *The Christian Faith and the Common Life.*
> *Church and Community.*
> *Church, Community and State in Relation to Education.*
> *The Universal Church and the World of Nations.*

On the subject of the relation of the Church to the State a volume by Mr. Nils Ehrenström is being published by the Student Christian Movement Press under the title *Christian Faith and the Modern State.* This may be regarded as in many respects supplementary to the present volume. Another valuable contribution to the same subject, also prepared with the Oxford Conference in view, is *Church and State in Contemporary America,* by Dr. William Adams Brown, published by Scribners.

The present volume has the advantage that it has grown out of several group discussions and that earlier drafts were submitted to a large number of persons for criticism. It suffers from the disadvantage that the writing of it has been controlled by a time-table. Comments on two successive drafts of a paper on the functions of the Church were received from nearly a hundred persons in different countries representing many different points of view. These comments, many of which ran to a considerable number of pages, contained a wealth of suggestion of which free use has been made. It is impossible to make acknowledgment by name to those who have given such generous help. Without this help the shortcomings of the volume would be even greater than they are. The chapters by Dr. Visser 't Hooft were similarly read and commented on by a number of critics. On the other hand, it is not the ideal way to produce a good book to have to send the earlier chapters to the press before the later ones are written. This was unavoidable, however, if faith was to be kept with the delegates to the Oxford Conference for whom the book was primarily written. The indulgence of readers is asked for blemishes which greater leisure for revision would have made it possible to remove.

Mr. Nils Ehrenström spent two or three weeks with me while the volume was being prepared and collaborated in the writing of Chapter VI on "The Church and the World" and the final chapter on "The Spring of Christian Action." Without the help of his wide theological knowledge these chapters could not have been written, and considerable parts of them are from his hand.

I have to thank my colleagues, Mr. Eric Fenn and Miss Olive Wyon, for many helpful suggestions, and in particular for reading the proof and preparing the index.

It is not an easy task to do justice to the different tendencies in Christian thought on the subject of the Church and its functions in society. This volume does not profess to accomplish what must be the task of many years. Its aim is not to put forward conclusions but to initiate and stimulate discussion. It will serve its purpose if, in spite of many imperfections in the execution,·it helps in some measure to clarify the issues and to direct attention to questions with which Christian thought must concern itself in the years to come.

J. H. OLDHAM

PART I

THE OCCASION AND THE SETTING

by

Dr. J. H. OLDHAM

THE OCCASION AND THE SETTING

FOR those who hold, or are held by, the Christian faith, and who are moved by Christian compassion for the distresses, frustrations, and anxieties of mankind, no more momentous question can be posed for consideration than the question how the Church can bear its witness, fulfil its mission, and be the messenger of God's redeeming mercy to the world. The assembling together at Oxford of representatives of the Church from all parts of the world to examine this question and to face this responsibility is an occasion that must quicken hope. The fruitfulness of the deliberations depends, however, on the measure in which the issues at stake are apprehended in their true gravity. It is a vital question whether the Conference deals with them at a superficial level, or pierces to their real depths.

There is a widespread sense, which finds expression in the writings and utterances of many serious thinkers, Christian and non-Christian, that we stand to-day at one of the major turning-points in history. The basal assumptions which have hitherto given a meaning to life, and unity and stability to civilization, have lost their unquestioned validity. An epoch in the life of mankind is drawing to a close, and we are on the threshold of a new age in which new conceptions of life still struggling in the womb of time will rule men's minds and direct their conduct. We are not concerned here to enquire how far and in what sense these assertions are true. It is not the task of the Conference at Oxford to attempt to formulate a philosophy of history. What is important for our present purpose is the indubitable fact that we live in the midst of profound and far-reaching change. The relative stability of the world which existed before the war has gone. The foundations of human society are quivering. The fact itself none will dispute, but our minds become dulled by familiarity to its significance. We give it our indolent assent, and contentedly resume the tenor of our habitual attitudes. There can, however, be no true wrestling with the realities of the contemporary situation, except in so far as we allow their meaning to break through the crust of our customary thinking into those deeper levels of our being in which our experience is absorbed and organized, so that there will take place progressively, and to a large extent subconsciously, a reconstruction of our whole outlook, and a reorientation of our fundamental attitudes.

An openness of the mind and of the whole being to the realities of the world in which the mission of the Church has to be fulfilled to-day is essential, if the deliberations of the Oxford Conference are to be fruitful. For this will determine the scale and proportion of what is thought and said and done, and set the measure of our desires and expectations. It will make all the difference to the discussions whether the assumption, conscious or unexpressed, is that all that is needed to enable the Church to fulfil its mission is an extension and improvement of its present organization, activities, and methods; or whether we are willing that these familiar forms should give place, if God so will, to others more adequate to meet the needs of the present time, and are ready for the stream of Christian life to break out in fresh ways and create for itself new channels of expression. It is of no small moment whether when we speak of the Church we picture to ourselves the Church as we have hitherto known it, or whether we are thinking in trustful expectancy of the Church which it is in the power of God to fashion as the instrument for the fulfilment of His purpose in our time and in the days to come.

It is fitting that a conference meeting to consider the relations between the Church and the Community and the State should take as its starting-point a fresh consideration of the meaning of the Church and the nature of its mission. That the Church of Christ is the one hope of the world is the faith which we confess in meeting in conference at Oxford. But this faith, which is the master light of all our seeing, is far from warranting the conclusion that the same thing can be predicated of the Churches which send representatives to Oxford. We fall too easily into the mistake of equating God's purpose for the Church with what our limited understanding and imperfect embodiment of that purpose make of the Church as it actually exists. We believe that to the Church is entrusted the truth which has power to save the world, but this treasure, as St. Paul reminds us, is contained in vessels of clay. In the divine and human institution of the Church the human element is always tending to limit, and obscure, and even to deny the divine. God's way with men is to lead them to repentance, in order that being delivered from their corrupt and paralysing past they may serve Him in newness of life. A profound dissatisfaction with what the Church now is, with what it at present sees, with its present understanding of its message and its responsibilities is the spiritual soil in which the seeds of new life may germinate. It is when we have come to despair of ourselves that the divine mercy meets us, and we learn to put our whole trust and confidence in God.

In a gathering at the present time of representatives of the Church from different parts of the world there cannot be absent a sense of the responsibility of historical decision. A heightened appreciation of the significance of history is a characteristic of our time. Even in its secular forms, this owes doubtless more than it is often aware of to Christian thought. It is at least a view that is wholly congruous with the Christian understanding of life. For Christian faith is concerned from first to last with the mighty acts of God in human history. God is at work in history. He has a purpose in it, and He calls men to share in the fulfilment of that purpose. The fact that we live in history and form part of history implies that not only to prophets and heroes, but also to ordinary men there may come moments when important events may hinge on their choice and action. Through the issues which the Oxford Conference will consider God may be calling the Church to make up its mind whether it is content to follow beaten and well-tried paths, or is ready at His command to meet the unknown and uncertain future in fresh and bold adventures of faith.

PART II

THE CHURCH AND THE CHURCHES

by

Dr. W. A. VISSER 'T HOOFT

FOREWORD TO PART II

DURING the process of common thought and study which
has been in progress during the last few years on the
relations between Church, Community, and State, it
has become increasingly obvious that at the heart of
the whole discussion of these issues there is a question
of fundamental importance: "What is the nature
and mission of the Church with whose attitude to
social and political problems the Conference is concerned?" Unless there is an understanding in regard
to that basic question, the whole discussion must be
involved in confusion, and those who are participating
in the Conference at Oxford must find themselves at
cross-purposes.

It is not the specific task of the Oxford Conference to
consider that question with a view to the ultimate reunion
of the Churches. That is the special responsibility of the
Conference on Faith and Order which will meet a month
later in Edinburgh. But there are two reasons why the
Oxford Conference must face the problem of the Church.
One of these is that the real differences between the
various conceptions of the Church must be brought into
the open, so that the misunderstandings may be avoided
which would inevitably arise if it were taken for granted
that all the delegates used the word Church in the same
sense. The other one is that it must be made clear what
the Oxford Conference itself means when it speaks of the
Church.

This part of the present volume has therefore two main
objects: in the first place, to provide a brief survey of the
various meanings which are attached to the term Church
as used in oecumenical gatherings; and in the second
place, to attempt to answer these two questions: Is there

a Church in the Churches? And can the Churches speak and act together?

The first and second chapters deal with the various doctrinal conceptions of the Church, and with the Churches in History. This may seem a somewhat arbitrary division, but it has proved to be the only one which would make it possible to do justice to the two main sets of influences which have actually shaped the various conceptions of the Church and its relation to the world, namely, the theological and the sociological. A purely theological treatment would give a misleading impression of the real meaning which the word Church has to-day in many places. A purely sociological treatment would be even more misleading in that it would neglect the essential nature of the Church as a God-given community. The reality of the Church is always a tension between its divine intention and its actual life in the world, and in order to understand it both these aspects need to be taken into consideration. It is, of course, impossible for reasons of space to describe each individual Church from these two points of view, so the only possible solution seems to be to speak first of the main doctrinal conceptions of the Church, and then of the different historical situations in which the Churches find themselves to-day. In both cases I have, of course, been compelled to simplify the complexity of the real situation by dealing only with some of the main types, and by leaving out whatever seemed exceptional rather than typical. Even so, I do not claim that I have dealt adequately with the various conceptions of the Church, or with the various geographical situations. But I hope that the chapters may at least serve to demonstrate the immense variety of doctrine and of background which the Conference will have to take into account before it can start on its work of clarification.

This whole section on the various conceptions of the

Church, is meant to be purely descriptive. It is based largely on compilation from various sources, the most important of which are a document prepared by Dr. Oldham, and the comments on that document made by other collaborators in the preparation for the Conference.[1]

The third chapter, on "the Church as an Oecumenical Society," is of a somewhat different character. In it I have tried to indicate briefly what seem to be the main issues arising out of the variety in the doctrinal and historical backgrounds of the participating Churches, which should be faced by the Oxford Conference.

[1] Quotations without further bibliographical reference have generally been taken from memoranda which have been prepared in connection with the Conference at Oxford.

CHAPTER I

THE VARIOUS DOCTRINAL CONCEPTIONS
OF THE CHURCH

THE purpose of this chapter is to give a survey of the main doctrinal positions concerning the Church. In other words, the question to be answered in each case is: how does each Church, or group of Churches, understand itself, and its relation to the Church Universal? This inquiry will of necessity have to be based on representative utterances of the various Church bodies. In some cases the actual thought about the Church which is finding expression in preaching, in literature, and in action differs considerably from the official doctrinal position. But those cases will be dealt with in the next section on the "Churches in History."

Since it is quite impossible to enumerate and describe all particular Churches or denominations within the allotted space, it has been necessary to group all conceptions of the Church under some main headings. If some conceptions seem to be dealt with more fully, and others less fully, than seems justifiable in the light of their qualitative or quantitative significance, the reason is merely that it is necessary to bring out the distinctive traits and differences rather than the similarities. A short introductory section attempts to give a brief survey of the present position of New Testament studies concerning the Church.

I. THE COMMON APPEAL TO THE NEW TESTAMENT

All Christian Churches claim to have their roots in the New Testament. Their differences are therefore largely, though not wholly, based on differing interpretations of the New Testament conception of the Church, and of its faith and order. This common appeal to the New Testament represents, however, at the same time the dynamic element in the discussion between the Churches. For, in so far as the Churches not only use the New Testament to prove their particular claims but are willing to reconsider their doctrines in the light of their understanding of the New Testament, Biblical exegesis becomes a main agent in the oecumenical situation. The interpretation of the Bible is a historical process, during which times of far-reaching agreement are followed by times of disagreement or complete anarchy. And its influence upon the oecumenical situation varies accordingly. It is therefore worth while to ask at the outset of our discussion of the nature of the Church, how present-day Biblical scholarship affects our common thinking about the Church and its nature.

During the last fifty years a remarkable shift has taken place in regard to the understanding of the Church in the New Testament. In the eighties of the last century there was (at least among Protestant scholars) an almost general agreement in laying the emphasis on the conception of the Church as a religious association.[1] The devout Christian came first. He and his fellow-believers united in free association to create a congregation, and the Church was simply the conglomeration of such congregations. The whole conception of the Church was individualistic, democratic and atomistic. The New Testament Church was interpreted in terms of sociological and humanitarian ideas.

In the decades which followed, that view has been increasingly abandoned; but it is only in the last few

[1] See Olof Linton, *Das Problem der Urkirche in der neueren Forschung*, 1932.

years that something like a new consensus of opinion on the essential aspects of the New Testament Church has begun to form. Some of the main affirmations on which scholars of different countries and different confessions are to a large extent in agreement, are the following.

It is seen that the thought of the New Testament is governed by religious, and not by political categories, that the Church is built from above, and not from below, and has its source not in man, but in God. This interpretation implies the following main insights.

"The One Universal Church is primary, the local society expresses the life and unity of the whole,"[1] for "from the outset the Church was understood universally and each fraction of it was a 'Church' in so far as the part was a miniature of the whole."[2] Thus the Church is "a Body of men and women in which the unity of every part corresponds to, repeats, represents and in fact *is* the unity of the whole."[3]

The idea of the Church as used in the New Testament is a qualitative rather than a quantitative idea.[4] The Church exists where God calls His people together. It is not merely a new religious organization, but a new creation of God, and is therefore nothing less than the Church *of God*.

What this means becomes especially clear if one asks how the New Testament conceives of the relation between Christ and the Church. C. H. Dodd summarizes the ecclesiology of St. Paul in the following way: "It was not enough to say that Christ, being exalted to the right hand of God, had 'poured forth' the Spirit. The presence of

[1] A. M. Ramsey, *The Gospel and the Catholic Church*, 1936.
[2] E. F. Scott.
[3] Sir Edwyn Hoskyns, *The Riddle of the New Testament*, 1931.
[4] K. L. Schmidt, article "Ekklesia" in *Theologisches Wörterbuch zum Neuen Testament*.

the Spirit in the Church *is* the presence of the Lord:
'the Lord is the Spirit.' Thus the 'one body' which the
one Spirit created is the Body of Christ. To be 'in
the Spirit' is to be 'in Christ,' that is to say, a member
of the Body of Christ."[1] And K. L. Schmidt says that
St. Paul's ecclesiology is simply Christology, and *vice
versa.*[2]

At the same time recent scholarship has come to consider the Church as part of the primitive *kerugma.* C. H.
Dodd shows that the ideas of the Spirit in the Church
and of the calling of the Church as the Israel of God,
which are so prominent in the Pauline Epistles, are not
innovations of St. Paul, but part of the tradition which
he had received, that is, part of the Gospel common to
all or most early preachers.[3] And several, though by no
means all, New Testament scholars believe that the ver-
dict against the historical character of the passages in
Matthew xvi and xviii (the only ones in which the word
Ekklesia appears in Jesus' own teaching) should be
revised, and (or) that the Last Supper represents the
actual founding of the new Church.

But in spite of these important points of agreement,
there remain basic differences in interpretation. These
have to do especially with the meaning of the eschatological element in the New Testament conception of
the Church, and with the relation of that conception to
the later development of Catholicism.

That the New Testament Church should be understood
eschatologically is generally agreed. "The Church was
the society of the future age."[4] "The Church is the germ
of the Kingdom of God."[5] "The Church is necessary,
because the end is near."[6] But the question remains,

---

[1] *The Apostolic Preaching and its Developments*, 1936.
[2] Loc. cit.   [3] Loc. cit.   [4] E. F. Scott.
[5] Martin Dibelius.   [6] Olof Linton.

how this eschatology should be interpreted. Is this eschatology "realized eschatology" which implies a certain ontological identification between Christ and the Church, or is it "futurist eschatology" in the sense that the Church in this dispensation is essentially a waiting Church, which lives by the promise of the Kingdom of God? The answers given to this question depend, of course, on the answer given to the problem of the meaning of eschatology throughout the New Testament.

Some underline the presence of the supernatural life in the Church. Thus C. H. Dodd speaks of a "transformation" (in the thought of St. Paul) of "futurist eschatology" into a "Christ-mysticism," and says: "That supernatural order of life which the apocalyptists had predicted in times of pure fantasy is now described as an actual fact of experience. . . . In masterly fashion St. Paul has claimed the whole territory of the Church's life as the field of the eschatological miracle."[1] And L. S. Thornton says of the primitive Church: "In the place of that objective historical manifestation of divine love in terms of human life which they had seen in Christ they now possessed an interior presence of indwelling love in the fellowship of the Christian Community."[2] But others stress the fact that the Church is the community of those who live by faith and not by sight. Thus K. L. Schmidt says: "The Church is never *triumphans*, but only *militans*, that is to say, *pressa; ecclesia triumphans* would be the Kingdom of God, and no longer *ecclesia*."[3] And Hébert Roux: "The Church is in this fallen world, the body to which the grace has been given to hear and receive in faith the promise of the Kingdom of Christ. . . . At the end of His work of redemption which He has achieved and which is the restoration of the Kingdom, Christ returns

---

[1] *The Apostolic Preaching and its Developments*, 1936.
[2] In *Essays Catholic and Critical*, 1929.   [3] Loc. cit.

to His Father and shows thus that it remains for the Church to *believe* in the Kingdom. The Ascension inaugurates the time of the Church, the time of faith and of witness by the Holy Spirit."

The difference between these two views seems at first sight merely a difference in emphasis, but it may lead to far-reaching consequences. If the Church is primarily conceived as being in possession of supernatural life, it will be thought of as an "extension of the Incarnation," and as a body, the life and tradition of which carry a certain authority within themselves. On the other hand, if the Church is primarily viewed as existing "between the times," and the fundamental difference between the Church and the Kingdom is strongly underlined, it will be held that the Church remains exclusively dependent on the revelation in the New Testament message as "over against" its own life. In the same way the two views will lead to different conceptions of the attitude of the Church to the world, for the first view tends to emphasize the continuity between nature and grace and the progressive realization of the Kingdom in the world, while the second tends to emphasize the discontinuity between nature and grace and the transcendent and revolutionary character of the Kingdom.

Closely connected with this problem therefore is the other problem of the relations between the New Testament Church and the Catholic Church of the second and subsequent centuries. Just as there is considerable difference between scholars on the right interpretation of New Testament eschatology, so there is difference in this matter. But since a discussion of this issue leads automatically to a discussion of matters of Church order, which are not directly relevant to the subject of the Oxford Conference, it need not be dealt with here.

2. THE ROMAN CATHOLIC CHURCH

Although the Roman Catholic Church will not be officially represented at the Oxford Conference, its doctrine of the Church, both by the support which it lends in matters in which there is agreement, and by the contradiction which it provokes where there is disagreement, possesses a high degree of importance in the consideration of the relation of the Church to the social and political life of our time.

According to the definition of Bellarmin, the Church may be described as "a body of men united together by the profession of the same Christian faith and by participation in the same sacraments, under the governance of lawful pastors, more especially of the Roman pontiff, the sole Vicar of Christ on earth."

The Eternal Father in His eternal love has sent the Son into the world. It is man's duty to believe absolutely in this revelation and to obey the commandments of God. But in order to make this possible, Christ has founded His Church as a perfect society, external of its own nature and visible.[1] The incarnate Son of God has appointed the Pope, the Successor of St. Peter, as His representative, and conferred on him the threefold power to heal, to teach, and to govern. As Leo XIII declared in his Encyclical *Immortale Dei*: "The only-begotten Son of God established on earth a society which is called the Church, and to it He handed over the exalted and divine office which He had received from His Father, to be continued through the ages to come. Over this mighty multitude God has Himself set rulers with power to govern; and He has willed that one should be the head of all, and the chief and unerring teacher of truth, to whom He has given the keys of the Kingdom of Heaven. . . . Just as the end at which the Church aims is by far the noblest

[1] Encyclical *Mortalium Animos*.

of ends, so is its authority the most exalted of all authority, nor can it be looked upon as inferior to the civil power, or in any manner dependent upon it."

The Church is the vehicle both of the divine will and of the divine love. As the vehicle of the former it is a legal institution. Christ gave to the apostles and their successors authority to guide the Church, and they have made regulations to direct its life and work. These constitute the law of the Church. But this Church of law is at the same time a Church of love. The love of Christ accompanies the Church throughout its pilgrimage and constitutes it a community of love.

The spiritual character of the Church is strongly emphasized in the description of the nature of the Church proposed by the Commission of Theologians in preparation for the Vatican Council which would almost certainly have been adopted if the Council had not been suspended before the completion of its work. This description is based on the conception of the Church as the Body of Christ. "In order to describe the nature of the Church, it is determined according to the true and catholic teaching, that it is the mystical Body of Christ." Five reasons are given for this definition. Firstly, it is Biblical; secondly, it expresses the divine nature of the Church; thirdly, it shows that the Church is not only external; fourthly, only thus is the visible Church rightly understood, and lastly the spiritual view of the Church needs to be revived in the souls of the faithful at the present time.

Christ is not only the principle of the Church's external organization and visible unity, but also the life of its members; and in the Church His life has its continued expression. The Church is the reality of the new creation, which has been given by the Incarnation, and it is this in an ontological sense. There is in it and through it a true immanence of God in human life which expresses

itself in a way perceivable by man. "The Catholic *petra*
on which everything is based is the objective really visible
petra of the Church, and therefore the order of Supernature is independent of the ups and downs of human
subjects. . . . The Church is certainly the all in all of
Christ, but it is this, not in the invisibility of the continued life of the glorified Lord in heaven, that is to say:
eschatologically, but it is this as the foundation within
time of the God-man who came within time, in its institutional *gratia creata inhabitans*, which is for it the *Opus
Operatum* of the *Successio Apostolica*, based on the rock of
Peter; and it is this, not in a passive, but in an active
way, through the activity of the institutional unity of
divine and human law in its life."[1] This *inhabitatio* implies
that the Church is above all a Church of the Sacrament.
*"Per sacramenta omnis vera justitia vel incipit vel coepta augetur
vel amissa reparatur."*[2]

The Roman Catholic Church alone possesses the four
marks indicated in the Creed. The Church is *one*. This
implies that its form of government is monarchical, for
the papacy is the principle of unity. It is *holy*, because it
is the continuation of the life of Christ, because it represents God's Kingdom on earth, because its teaching,
priestly and pastoral ministry mediates the truth, grace
and love of Christ, and because the members of the
Church are members of the Body of Christ. It is also
Catholic or Universal, not merely in principle, but also in
actuality. Finally, it is *apostolic*. All ecclesiastical authority
is derived from the apostles, who have transmitted their
office to their lawful successors, and were themselves
appointed by Jesus Christ.[3]

[1] Erich Przywara, S.J., *Das Katholische Kirchenprinzip*, Zwischen
den Zeiten, 1929: 3.
[2] *Conc. Trid.*
[3] Ludwig Kösters, *Die Kirche unseres Glaubens*.

Since the Roman Catholic Church considers that "all other confessions have separated themselves from the Roman Church, which was founded directly by Christ," it holds that "Rome cannot go to them; it is for them to return to the Roman Church."[1] On the other hand, "everyone who has received baptism belongs somehow to the Pope" and to the Church[2] and thus Christians of other confessions, "though far from the visible centre, have a special claim on our love," and may be considered as brothers in Christ. In Roman Catholic theology this idea is sometimes elaborated in the form of a distinction between the body and the soul of the Church (the latter being visible only "to some extent"), or in the form of a distinction between explicit and implicit membership of the Church. The baptized Christian who is of good faith, and who does not consciously and arbitrarily oppose the truth of the Church, may "belong" to the Church. At the same time, there are those in the membership of the Church who do not really "belong" to it. In this sense, and in this sense only, it can be said that the eternal Church of Christ and the visible institution are not fully identical with each other.

The task of the Church is to carry forward the work of the Redeemer. The Church therefore seeks progressively to permeate both individuals and society with its supernatural powers. According to the teaching of St. Thomas Aquinas, the Church recognizes the polarity of man as a creature with certain natural powers, and also touched by and elevated to certain supernatural realities. Baron von Hügel defines this position as follows: "The leading categories are no more Sin and Redemption, but Nature and Supernature . . . The centrally natural life forms and finds its specific complex in the State; the centrally super-

---

[1] Statement concerning the Lausanne Conference, made in 1919.
[2] Letter of Pope Pius IX to Kaiser Wilhelm I in 1873.

natural life has its specific expression and means in the Church. The State is here recognized as being essentially ethical, although ethical in an elementary, homely, give-and-take, calculating and self-conscious way; and the Church has not to infuse *this* morality into the State, but has only to aid in awakening it there, as a morality already and always latent in the State as such. The Church has, roughly speaking, to begin where the State leaves off; and *its* ethics are of a transcending, abiding, self-oblivious, God-seeking and God-finding order, the whole a gift from the God of Grace."[1] Or, in the words of the Encyclical *Immortale Dei:* "The Almighty has appointed the charge of the human race between two powers, the ecclesiastical and civil, the one being set over divine, the other over human things." The Church recognizes the authority of the State in its own legitimate sphere, but cannot remain indifferent to the import of the laws enacted by the State, since God has assigned to the Church the duty, not only of resisting actions of the State which run counter to religion, but also of making "a strong endeavour that the power of the gospel may pervade the laws and institutions of the nations." It must be reckoned among the duties of Christians that "they allow themselves to be ruled and directed by the authority and leadership of bishops, and above all of the Apostolic See . . . Both what we are bound to believe, and what we are obliged to do, are laid down by the Church using her divine right."

3. THE EASTERN ORTHODOX CHURCH

While the Roman Catholic Church is to a very large extent an institutional and legal body, the Orthodox Church is not in the first place an institution, but a worshipping community and a life in Christ, guided by

[1] Friedrich von Hügel, *The German Soul*, 1916.

the Holy Spirit. Orthodoxy shares with Roman Catholicism the acceptance of tradition as an organ of divine revelation; but it means by tradition "the truths which came down from Our Lord and the Apostles through the Fathers, which are confessed unanimously and continuously in the Undivided Church;"[1] and since it has no continuously-functioning agency for the interpretation of tradition, it does not present its doctrine in the form of a closed and detailed system.

It is therefore not always easy to describe the Eastern Orthodox position concerning matters which were not defined authoritatively by the Oecumenical Councils of the early centuries. The conception of the Church is a case in point. Let us first describe the area of broad agreement.

The Eastern Orthodox view of the Church is inseparably bound up with the doctrine expressed in the well-known phrase of Athanasius that "Christ became man in order that we might become divine." The Church may therefore be described as "heaven on earth." An oft-repeated phrase in the liturgy is: "As we stand in the house of Thy glory, it is as though we stood in heaven itself." Or, in the words of Professor Florovsky: "The objective side (of the Church) is the uninterrupted sacramental succession, the continuity of the hierarchy. . . . The subjective side is loyalty to the apostolic tradition; a life spent according to this tradition, as in a living realm of truth. . . . The catholic nature of the Church is seen most vividly in the fact that the experience of the Church belongs to all times. In the life and existence of the Church time is mysteriously overcome and mastered; time, so to speak, *stands still.* . . . The Church is the living image of eternity within time."[2]

[1] *Report of the Joint Doctrinal Commission* appointed by the Oecumenical Patriarch and the Archbishop of Canterbury, 1932.
[2] In *The Church of God,* 1934.

The Church is the mystical and sacramental unity of all believers, past, present, and future, with one another and with the only Head of the Church, Jesus Christ. The bishops are successors of the apostles; and this fact constitutes the apostolic character of the Church; for thus the Church "preserves teaching and discipleship without change and without interruption as gifts of the Holy Spirit through holy ordination." The Church as the body in which Christ is eternally present is infallible. "Christ, the Head of the Church which is His Body, is its Lifegiver and its Leader, so that it is impossible for it to fall into error; for He is the Truth itself. . . . An individual Bishop or a particular local Church may err, but the Church as a whole is infallible."[1]

That the hierarchy has spiritual and pastoral authority is general Orthodox doctrine. But there are various conceptions of the character and limits of that authority. One view, which appeals to statements of Orthodox synods and official catechisms, maintains that the hierarchy has a special authority in matters of doctrine, and that this authority is not derived from the consensus of the faithful. Another view, which was formulated by Khomiakov in the nineteenth century, but which claims to be an explanation of what the Orthodox Church has actually been in its history, holds that the Eastern Church does not recognize any formal, external or juridical authority, because the Church itself, and not any part of it, is infallible. It believes that the "guardian of piety is the body of the Church, that is, the people itself,"[2] and that dogmatic utterances of Councils and synods "have their significance, not in the fact that they possess an infallible authority in matters of faith (which they do not possess),

---

[1] Chrysostomos, Archbishop of Athens, at the Lausanne Conference.
[2] Letter of the Orthodox Patriarchs to Pope Pius IX.

but in the fact that they are means for the articulation
and expression of the consciousness of the Church"
(Bulgakov)[1] This consciousness of the whole Church,
expressed through the unity of its members (in Russian
their *sobornost*), is thus the true criterion of truth, and has
absolute authority. It expresses itself not only in the
doctrine, but above all in the liturgy, of the Church. It
is obvious that this conception stands in opposition to
the Roman Catholic conception which (according to the
Vatican Council) ascribes to dogmatic decisions of the
Pope an authority which resides in themselves and not
in the consensus of the faithful (*ex sese, non autem ex
consensu ecclesiae*). On the other hand, it is also different
from the Reformation position, according to which the
final authority is not the Church, but the Holy Scriptures. The *sobornost* theology has not been formulated
explicitly and accepted by the Church as a whole, and
represents therefore a *theologoumenon* rather than an
official position.[2]

The attitude of the Orthodox Church to other Churches
is characterized by a combination of two convictions. On
the one hand, the Orthodox Church is the true Church,
the one holy catholic and apostolic Church which is confessed in the Creed. On the other hand, it recognizes
other Churches as real, though imperfect parts of the
Body of Christ. Thus the Orthodox delegates at the
Lausanne Conference of "Faith and Order" declared
that no reunion could be achieved except on the basis of
the common faith of the undivided Church of the seven
oecumenical councils. But at the same time, the Oecumenical Patriarch, in his Encyclical of 1920, proposed closer
intercourse between the several Christian Churches, an

[1] Bulgakov, quoted by Heiler in *Urkirche und Ostkirche*, 1937.
[2] The Metropolitan of Thyateira in *Joint Doctrinal Commission
Report*.

intercourse "which is not prevented by the doctrinal differences existing between them;" and the Orthodox Churches co-operate fully with the different oecumenical movements. Sacramental unity can be realized only on the basis of dogmatic agreement; but collaboration in common Christian tasks is possible in the meantime.

In its attitude to the world, the Orthodox Church thinks in terms of penetrating this world from within rather than in terms of changing it outwardly. This is often expressed by the term: the "Churchification" or transfiguration of the world, which means that the supernatural life of the Church should permeate the whole life of society. In view of its strong belief in the cosmic character of the revelation, which enables it to see symbols of Christian truth in many aspects of nature and society, the Orthodox Church does not draw a sharp distinction between the sacred and the secular.

4. THE ANGLICAN COMMUNION

The Anglican Communion harbours within itself the most widely different doctrines of the Church. Its comprehensiveness in this respect is one of its distinguishing characteristics. It claims to be both Catholic and Protestant. The Lambeth Conference of 1930 stated: "Our special character and, as we believe, our peculiar contribution to the Universal Church, arises from the fact that, owing to historic circumstances, we have been enabled to combine in our one fellowship the traditional Faith and Order of the Catholic Church with that immediacy of approach to God through Christ to which the Evangelical Churches especially bear witness, and freedom of intellectual inquiry, whereby the correlation of the Christian revelation and advancing knowledge is constantly effected." Or in the words of the Archbishop of York: "We can hold out a hand both to the ancient Churches of the East and to Rome on the one side, and to all those who with us are heirs of the Reformation on the other; and in that we have a position unique in Christendom, the full value of which can only be realized for the Universal Church so far as we are true to both sides of our own tradition."[1]

The Anglican Communion often appears to the outsider as a house divided against itself, for it contains different parties or groupings whose fundamental convictions seem to contradict each other. But as the Bishop of Chichester has pointed out in his "Brief Sketch of the Church of England:" "Every party is, as such, a minority, and all the parties together are still a minority of Church members. The great multitude of those who belong to the Church of England, though helped by all are tied by none. And all are bound together by the fourfold cord: the Episcopate, the Bible, the Prayer Book and the Crown, that is, in the language of an earlier day, the Christian Prince." With the exception of the reference to the Crown, these words are equally applicable to the other Churches of the Anglican communion.

There are in the Anglican Communion representatives of several of the conceptions of the Church which are described in the various other sections of this chapter. But there is at the same time a conception which is truly characteristic of Anglicanism and which constitutes as it were its main line of development. This conception has been variously described as the theory of comprehensiveness or the *via media*. It is a Catholic ideal, in that it conceives of the body of Christ as consisting of very different types of members, each useful in their own way, and none to be glorified at the expense of the others. It is also Catholic in the more substantial sense of the word, in that it receives its inspiration from a faith in the con-

[1] *Essays in Christian Politics.*

tinuous and common tradition of the living Christian Church.

The Lambeth Conference of 1930 approved the following statement of the nature and status of the Anglican Communion:—

"The Anglican Communion is a fellowship, within the One Holy Catholic and Apostolic Church, of those duly constituted Dioceses, Provinces or Regional Churches in communion with the See of Canterbury, which have the following characteristics in common—

(a) they uphold and propagate the Catholic and Apostolic faith and order as they are generally set forth in the Book of Common Prayer as authorized in their several Churches;

(b) they are particular or national Churches, and, as such, promote within each of their territories a national expression of Christian faith, life and worship; and—

(c) they are bound together not by a central legislative and executive authority, but by mutual loyalty sustained through the common counsel of the Bishops in Conference."

"Protestant" in its insistence on the truth that "Holy Scripture containeth all things necessary to salvation," "Catholic" in its estimate of tradition and of the main guardian of tradition which is the Episcopate, it looks upon the Church as "the organ through which the Spirit now finds expression in the world,"[1] or, as many younger Anglicans would put it, as "an extension of the Incarnation." The visible Church has therefore definite spiritual authority. "By the guidance of the Holy Spirit residing in the Church" Holy Scripture is "completed, explained, interpreted and understood,"[2] and this authority resides

[1] Lambeth Encyclical, 1930.
[2] Joint Doctrinal Report.

above all in the liturgical tradition.[1] For the same reason it attaches very great importance to the order of the Church, for "it is part of the life that is always going on," and particularly to the Episcopate, for it is "the natural source (on earth) of teaching, discipline and ministration of the sacraments."[2]

But if the Church is already Catholic in principle, it must work for the realization of that full Catholicity which means nothing less than the reunion of all Christendom into one visible and united body. A purely spiritual and invisible unity or a purely "intensive" Catholicity is not enough. Unity must find expression in a common Faith and Order, and both terms are equally important.

Thus it is no mere accident that the Anglican Churches are more active than any other Churches in the movement for the reunion of the Christian Churches. Their visible unity is an essential element in their whole conception of the Church, and the conception of the Church is at the same time influenced by the desire for unity. They stand in the centre of a process of conversations and negotiations with Churches as different from each other as the Eastern Orthodox Church and several Protestant Churches. And they are hopeful that out of this process there may emerge some day a world-wide Church which will contain both the Catholic and the Protestant traditions just as to-day the Anglican Church "includes inevitably the Scriptures and the salvation of the individual; as inevitably the order and the sacramental life of the Body of Christ, and the freedom of thought wherewith Christ has made men free."[3]

In its attitude to the world, the Anglican Church con-

---

[1] The Prayer Book is more authoritative than the Thirty-nine Articles; see Joint Doctrinal Report.

[2] S. C. Carpenter in *Towards Reunion*, 1934.

[3] A. M. Ramsey, *The Gospel and the Catholic Church*, 1936.

tains all shades of opinion, ranging from extreme pietism
and conservatism to social activism and Christian communism. But here again the main guiding principle is
not to be identified with any extreme position. For the
typically Anglican attitude to the world is, neither to
accept the world as it is, nor to revolutionize it from top
to bottom, but rather to hold that the world is gradually
to be permeated by the Spirit of God. No sharp distinctions are drawn between the transcendent and the
immanent, but neither are the two identified. Thus the
Lambeth Encyclical of 1930 speaks of the "perfecting of
humanity in Jesus Christ" as "the attainment of the purpose of the whole cosmic process through the agency of
the immanent Logos or creative thought of God." God
is "the Great Educator" who changes human nature.
But side by side with this optimistic evolutionary conception, there is also another more critical view, which
finds nourishment in the more eschatological piety of the
Prayer Book. The Anglican Church seems sometimes a
Church which merely consecrates the world; but it can
also turn against the world in order to proclaim a message
of judgment. It is a Catholic Church with Protestant
elements, and it is a priestly Church with prophetic
elements.

5. THE LUTHERAN CHURCHES

The early formulations of Lutheran doctrine contain
strong statements concerning the necessity of the Church
for salvation. According to the Greater Catechism the
Church is "the mother which through the Word of God
gives birth to every Christian and supports him."

The Lutheran conception of the Church finds its classic
expression in the Augsburg Confession, where the Church
is defined as "the congregation of saints in which the

Gospel is purely taught, and the sacraments rightly administered." This conception implies that the Word and the Sacraments actually constitute the Church, and that they are always efficacious, either for salvation or for judgment. The Word of God is given in Holy Scripture, but it must at the same time be preached. Holy Scripture is therefore the source of the Church's witness, its basis, and the "unique rule and norm, according to which all doctrine and all teachers should be estimated and judged."[1]

Tradition has its value, but it should not be co-ordinated with Holy Scripture. For tradition is merely human, and wherever it is accepted on a footing of equality with Scripture, it leads to a confusion between that which is of God and that which is of men. The Church is not to govern Scripture, but to be obedient to it.

The two basic marks of the Church, which are at the same time the creative powers which build the Church, are: the Word and the Sacraments. The Lutheran Church has no official doctrinal position concerning matters of Church order. There is one indispensable ministry: the ministry of the Word of God and the Sacraments, which is a divine institution, but the constitution and the discipline of the Church are considered as matters of secondary importance, which should not be confused with matters of faith. Indeed, it is held that if matters of order are put on the same level as the Word and the Sacraments, the Gospel is transformed into a new law, and the preaching of the Gospel, the heart of which is the message of justification and the remission of sins, is no longer "pure." It is for this reason that there is great diversity among the Lutheran Churches as regards their constitution, and that those Lutheran Churches which are in possession of "valid orders" (in the Catholic sense

[1] Formula of Concord.

of that term) do not attach any doctrinal significance to that fact, and do not consider the episcopacy as one of the indispensable marks of the Church.

The Church as the community of believers is hidden, in so far as the members of Christ are only known to God. It is, however, not an invisible, or a merely ideal reality, for the faithful can recognize it by the presence of the means of grace. There is room for a distinction between an *ecclesia proprie dicta* (the "inner Christendom") and an *ecclesia late dicta* (the "outer Christendom"), but this distinction does not coincide with Calvin's distinction between the visible and the invisible Church, for the means of grace are necessarily efficacious, and by them the Church is recognizable for faith as an actuality in the world. In later Lutheran theology, and to-day in several Lutheran Churches, the distinction between the visible and the invisible Church is, however, used to explain the twofold nature of the Church as a divine and a human reality.[1] Thus the Church of Sweden states: "This Church is from one point of view an inward fellowship of faith and love, which in the unity of the Spirit binds together all children of God in heaven and on earth, with God and with one another. From the other point of view, the same Church is a community, organized in changing outward forms, for the ministration of the means of grace, by which Christ, through the Holy Spirit, reconciles men to God, kindling faith, granting the remission of sins, and bringing their wills into subjection to His Sovereignty, so as to unite them in love and service of God and men, and to make them Christ's witnesses and fellow-workers in the extension of God's rule on earth until His Kingdom come in glory."[2]

[1] See, e.g., the answers of the various Lutheran Churches to the Report of the Lausanne Conference in *Convictions*.
[2] Ibid.

With regard to its oecumenical attitude the Lutheran Church distinguishes sharply between matters of faith and matters of order. The Augsburg Confession states: "For the Church's true unity it is sufficient to be one in the preaching of the Word and in the administration of the Sacraments. But it is not necessary that everywhere there be the same human traditions or such forms and ceremonies as are appointed by men." The Lutheran Church is therefore willing to acknowledge all Church forms as valid, and conceives of the process toward re-union as the endeavour "to fill those forms that already exist with a clear, rich, evangelical Christian content, and to remove anything through which the Gospel itself might be overshadowed, so that in this way an approach may be possible between the Churches also in their outward forms."[1]

On the other hand, the confessions of faith have a greater place in the Lutheran Churches than in most other Protestant Churches. Thus the Formula of Concord claims to be a "solid testimony, not only to those who live now, but also to all posterity." In matters of faith, therefore, the Lutheran Churches often take an uncompromising stand against any attempts to arrive at doctrinal agreement at the expense of their main articles of faith. Fundamentally all Lutheran Churches and theological schools agree that the content of the Confessions needs to be continually tested by the Word of God as the unique rule and norm of faith. But there is difference of opinion as to whether every single article, if measured by this norm, should be maintained or whether the present understanding of the Word of God demands new formulations. There is, however, one article which is *articulum stantis aut cadentis ecclesiae*, namely, justification by faith alone.

The Lutheran Church recognizes that the true Church

---

[1] Church of Norway in *Convictions*.

is also present in other particular Churches. *Ubi Christus, ibi ecclesia.* Wherever, in any of the other Churches, Christ is present, there the Church *is.* Lutherans believe that "those people are the true Church, who all over the world, from the rising of the sun to the going down of the same, believe truly in Christ, who have the one gospel, one Christ, one baptism, and one sacrament, who are governed by one Holy Spirit, even if they have different ceremonies."[1]

Lutheran social ethics are based on the doctrine of the divine orders, orders which God has ordained in order to conserve the world until the last judgment. These orders include the orders of nature, of creation, of family and work, and of government. The Gospel does not do away with these orders. "The Gospel teaches not an outward, temporal, but an inward, eternal attitude and righteousness of the heart, and does not overthrow worldly authority, civil force and order of marriage, but rather desires that all these should be accepted as the true order, and that everyone should show Christian love and good works according to his own calling and vocation."[2]

It is, however, a condition of obedience that the government should be a legitimate government, which fulfils its duty to protect justice and to keep the peace. If this is not the case, government becomes tyranny, and will be judged by God. The Church can refuse obedience, if it is asked to condone or to commit sin.

In addition to the calling of the father and of the government, there is the calling of the ministry. Its task is the preaching of the Word which includes the *usus legis politicus* (that is to say, the teaching concerning the orders and commandments of God concerning society). The realms of the Church and of the government should not

---

[1] Apologia of the Augsburg Confession.
[2] Augsburg Confession.

be confused,[1] because the Gospel and the Law should not be confused. The reign of Christ is hidden until the coming of the Kingdom of God (*tectum cruce*). It is there where the Word and the Sacrament are present, but it can only be recognized by faith.

Thus in original Lutheranism, and in much of present-day Lutheranism, there is a strong eschatological strain, which tends to a realistic acceptance of the main orders of this world as the inevitable form of human relationships in a sinful world, but which does not exclude a very high social morality on the part of individuals, and a consciousness of the duty of the Church to demand that the authorities should obey the Will of God. On the other hand, it should not be forgotten that there have been many Lutheran Churchmen and theologians who, while accepting the full tension between the law of love and social realities, have been pioneers in social ethics and action. Lutheranism remains, however, opposed to all forms of Christian activism which would apply the law of love *directly* to politics or social life. For it considers that such "spiritualism" fails to recognize the true calling of the State and the nature of our present sinful human situation.

6. THE REFORMED CHURCHES

The group of Churches which owe their origin to the Reformation in Switzerland and France have never had a common confession of faith such as the Lutheran Churches have in the Augsburg Confession. This is partly due to the fact that the "Reformed" Reformation has several different sources and partly to the fact that the Confessions of Faith, according to Reformed doctrine,

---

[1] *Non igitur commiscendae sunt potestates ecclesiastica et civilis*, Augsburg Confession.

have a concrete and historical rather than a general and permanent significance. They are provisional statements of the teachings of a given Church, which can and should be tested again and again in the light of God's present and actual Word, spoken through Holy Scripture, which alone is the "infallible rule," and to which "no human documents, however holy they may have been, should be compared" (*Confessio Belgica*, Art. vii).

To-day some Reformed Churches have no confession at all, some have confessions drawn up more or less recently, and some hold to the confessions of the sixteenth and seventeenth centuries.

There are, however, a number of points concerning the nature of the Church in which the Reformed Churches, in so far as they have not broken completely with their historical origins, are still at one. These points are found in practically all the historic Reformed confessions of faith, and are being taught to-day by Reformed theologians in many different countries.

It has been said that "among the Reformed, dogmatics is a '*locus*' in the Church; while among the Lutherans, the Church is a '*locus*' in dogmatics."[1] This statement is somewhat too clever to be true, but it points to an important difference between the two confessions. In Calvinist theology, the *Soli Deo Gloria* leads to a co-ordination of faith *and* obedience, of justification *and* sanctification which differs from the exclusive emphasis on justification by faith in Lutheranism. Calvinism follows Lutheranism in its emphasis on the objective, "given" character of the Church as the body which offers God's Word and God's Grace to men; but it qualifies the Lutheran conception by emphasizing strongly that the Church is also the *holy Community* which in its life must demonstrate that

[1] Hundeshagen. Quoted by Ernst Troeltsch in *Soziallehren*, 1919.

"God has created the world in order that it might be the theatre of His Glory."[1]

The characteristics of the Reformed conception of the Church are therefore the following:—

In the first place, the Reformed faith gives a very central place to the Church. "Whosoever departs from the Church denies God and Jesus Christ," says Calvin.[2]

In the second place the Reformed Churches distinguish between the visible and the invisible Church, but this distinction does not imply a separation between these two aspects of the Church. "As it is necessary that we should believe in the Church, invisible to us and known to one only, God; so it has been commanded that we should honour the visible Church and remain in communion with it." And "everywhere that we see the Word of God purely preached and listened to, and the sacraments administered according to the institution of Christ, we must never doubt that there is the Church."[3] Calvinism, while never taking it for granted that a given Church as such is in its own right and necessarily the Church of God, or that the Church carries any authority within itself, believes nevertheless that *in faith*, that is in the attitude of constant willingness to receive God's Grace anew, men may be assured that they are within the Church of God.

The Church is visible in the sense that it has characteristics which can be recognized in faith (the preaching of the Word and the Sacraments), but it is invisible in that it is the "society of those whom God has chosen to save, which cannot fully be perceived by our eyes."[4] The Church depends therefore at every moment upon God's present grace. It lives, not by itself, but by the strength of the promises of God. The Church does not "possess" the truth, but receives the truth of God again and again.

[1] Calvin.
[2] *Institutes* IV, 1, 10.
[3] *Institutes* IV, 1, 7, and 9.
[4] Geneva Catechism of 1545.

In the third place, the Reformed Churches take a more critical, or as its critics would say, a more iconoclastic attitude towards tradition. In view of their mistrust of human institutions, the Reformed Churches attach no value to the temporal continuity of ecclesiastical tradition, and reject, not only what is against Scripture, but also what seem to them to be human additions to Scripture.

In the fourth place, the Reformed conception of the nature of the Church includes a conviction with regard to Church discipline and the order of the Church (at this point the characteristic Calvinistic emphasis on the Church as a *Christian Community* finds expression). Though it cannot be said that Church discipline has been considered by all Reformed Confessions and teachers as a *nota ecclesiae*, it has generally been regarded as an indispensable characteristic of the true Church.[1] At the same time, several (not all) Reformed Confessions speak of the Presbyterian order as the "order which our Lord Jesus Christ has established,"[2] and thus consider the question of the Church's constitution as a point of doctrine rather than a matter of expediency. To-day several Churches of the Reformed tradition would no longer hold to this article of faith. The Church of Scotland holds the Presbyterian polity to be "agreeable to the Word of God" without claiming for it a *de jure* or exclusive divine authority. The Presbyterian Church in the U.S.A. holds that its order is expedient and agreeable to Scripture, but adds: "We embrace, in the spirit of charity, those Christians who differ from us, in opinion, and practice, on these subjects." And the Presbyterian Church of Wales goes much farther by saying: "It (the Assembly) does not believe that one particular form of ministry is divinely instituted and is for that reason immutable."[3]

[1] Thus, e.g., *Confessio Belgica*, 29.
[2] *Conf. Gallicana*, 29.
[3] *Convictions.*

In their attitude to other Churches the Reformed Churches differ very considerably. The common conviction is that "the visible Church, which is also Catholic or universal under the Gospel (not confined to one nation as before under the law), consists of all those throughout the world that profess the true religion, together with their children; and is the Kingdom of the Lord Jesus Christ, the house and family of God, out of which there is no ordinary possibility of salvation."[1] But some Reformed Churches would interpret "the true religion" as the full faith, expressed in the historic confessions, while others are ready to interpret these words in an extremely broad manner. The Reformed Churches do not insist on agreement in "outward rites and ceremonies," but rather in "the truth and unity of the Catholic faith;"[2] but while some go to the extreme of refusing all collaboration with other Churches who do not define the Christian faith in exactly the same manner as they do themselves, others go to the opposite extreme of a latitudinarian attitude in matters of doctrine.

The attitude of the Reformed Churches to the world follows from their conception of the Church. Since the Church is not concerned only with the proclamation of the message of Grace, but also with the response given to that message in the life of the faithful, it gives guidance in matters of public as well as private life. That does not mean that the Church takes the place of the State; for the State has its own God-given task. (Among the early Calvinists this task was conceived as "repressing the sins committed, not only against the second table of the commandments of God, but also against the first,"[3] but to-day few Reformed Churches hold that the State should intervene in spiritual and religious matters.) The

---

[1] Westminster Confession.
[2] Second Helvetic Confession.   [3] *Conf. Gallicana.*

Church "is subject to no civil authority,"[1] and it has
the right and the duty to give direction to its members
through its discipline in all matters of morality, private
and public, and to demand that the State should obey
the law of God. Since the law of God is given, not only
to bring men to repentance, but also to restrain the wicked,
and (*tertius usus legis*) to reveal the Will of God to believers,
the Reformed Church seeks in the Bible the principles
according to which the social and political order should
be organized. Thus the Reformed faith has always had
a strong sense of its mission in public life, and has in
many countries become a force of social and political
renewal and transformation. It does not believe, however,
that any particular human society can ever correspond
to the Kingdom of God, for it is aware of the eschatological
boundary to all human activity. "Though Jesus Christ
offers us in the Gospel a true and real fullness of all
spiritual gifts, the enjoyment of these is still hidden under
the guardianship and the seal of hope."[2] It must, however, be added that in modern times the Reformed
Churches have often forgotten this warning.

7. OTHER DEVELOPMENTS IN PROTESTANTISM

Although we find several of the largest single groups of
Christians among those Protestant Churches which can
be classified neither as Lutheran nor as Reformed, we
will take them together, partly because of lack of space,
and partly because their various conceptions of the Church
are related to each other.

The first main group is that of the *Congregational
Churches*. These belong in one sense to the Reformed
family, for their theology is largely based on Calvinism.
But they have also been influenced by Anabaptism, and

[1] Church of Scotland Act.   [2] *Institutes* II, 9, 3.

thus they lay greater stress upon the Christian *experience* of the individual believer. In England Congregationalism has stood for the conception of the "Gathered Church" in distinction from the national Churchmanship of the Church of England. A "Gathered Church" is a company of definitely committed believers.

Thus only local associations of experiential Christians are visible Churches, and of each of these Christ is the immediate and only Head. The local Church is therefore a completely self-governing body. "Such organization is preferable, as it allows the Church in each place and time to follow most freely the guidance of the Spirit."[1]

Congregationalism was "independent" in England, but "established" in New England, which shows that it did not break completely with the old notion of the all-embracing Church.

The *Baptists*, however, went further in the more subjective direction. The Baptist community stands partly in the Calvinist tradition, but it was also influenced by the Anabaptist sects on the Continent of Europe, and holds a conception of the Church which takes the Christian experience of the individual believer as its basis. For this reason baptism is restricted to persons who make an individual and personal surrender to Christ. The immediacy and inward character of the relation between God and man is emphasized; and the Church can never bring men into ordinary communion with God without personal faith. Some Baptists would say that the Church, while "essential for the perfection of Christian character, is not necessary to establish communion between God and men;"[2] but others would qualify this statement.

In view of their emphasis on religion as a personal relation between God and the soul, the Baptists reject

---

[1] Congregational Union of England and Wales in *Convictions*.
[2] Dr. Ashworth at the Lausanne Conference.

State control. The Baptists have been protagonists of religious tolerance, or, as Roger Williams called it, "soul liberty." It should be noted that a very similar conception of the Church is held by the *Disciples of Christ*.

The most consistently "inward" conception of the Church is certainly that of the *Quakers*. Their belief in the "inner light" has led them to reject all external forms of worship, and particularly the sacraments and the ordained ministry. "The claims of the inward light demanded a separation from all that was outward in religion, and left no place for a man-made ministry, or for reliance on the external features of Baptism and the Lord's Supper."[1] Their conception of the Church is therefore that it is "the fellowship of all sincere disciples of Jesus united in the life and experience of His continued presence with them as the Holy Spirit—united for the primary end of helping to establish His Kingdom in the world, and (incidentally to this) for nourishing His life in their souls by corporate worship."[2] All tradition, including the Bible itself, should be made subordinate to the continuing life of the Spirit which men come to know through their "inward Teacher."

The conception of the Church held by *Methodism* is difficult to describe, because Methodism has grown up as a revival movement, and because its standard of faith consists, not in confessions, but in sermons and commentaries. The statement on doctrine of the Methodist Church in England which was drawn up in 1932 at the time of the union of three Methodist Churches declares "that in the Providence of God Methodism was raised up to spread Scriptural Holiness through the land by the proclamation of the Evangelical Faith," that "the Methodist Church holds the doctrine of the priesthood

---

[1] *Beginnings of Quakerism.*
[2] Society of Friends in Great Britain in *Convictions.*

of all believers, and consequently believes that no priesthood exists which belongs exclusively to a particular order or class of men," and that "for the sake of Church order, and not because of any priestly virtue inherent in the office, the Ministers of the Church are set apart by ordination to the Ministry of the Word and Sacraments." The Methodist Episcopal Church in the United States of America has stated (in 1924) that "the historic notes of emphasis in Methodism have been on conversion, on entire sanctification, on the capture of the child life from earliest infancy for the Kingdom of Heaven, on the right of way of the spiritual interests over all ecclesiastical organization." Thus Methodism conceives of the Church as the fellowship growing out of the Christian experience of individuals. At the same time the other note of the Church as a God-given institution is not lacking. The 1932 Declaration says: "The Methodist Church claims and cherishes its place in the Holy Catholic Church, which is the Body of Christ." Thus the Methodist Church can be best described as "an attempt to combine institutionalism and individualism, stressing both the necessity of personal conversion and the importance of the institution of the Church."[1]

It is typical of the denominations described in this section that in their attitude to other Churches they demand first of all genuine Christian experience, and secondly the largest possible liberty of interpretation of the meaning of creeds, sacraments, and ministry, rather than uniformity of order or the adoption of the same confessions. This attitude is based on the conviction that the Church is essentially a community of believers rather than a community of belief, that is of corporate faith. In the language of Troeltsch, they are not so much Churches as "sects," which does not mean that they are more

[1] Cyril Richardson.

"sectarian" than other Christian groups, but that the voluntary element in their structure is stronger than the institutional one.

With regard to their attitude to the world, these four groups of Churches have shared in the Calvinist tradition of active participation in social and public life. The Congregationalists have given shape to New England Puritanism, which in turn has influenced the whole life of America. Their idea of the "Covenant" is one of the roots of modern democracy. The Baptists have been particularly influential through their stand for religious freedom, and paved the way for the separation of Church and State. The Quakers, though originally they were mainly a sect protesting against the ways of the world, have become pioneers in matters of social justice, and particularly in international understanding and pacifism. And the Methodists, who have always emphasized the moral claim in their evangelism, have more recently become very active in the realm of social justice. It is interesting to note that these four denominations have given the most cordial reception to that particular theology which is characterized by an active concern for the transformation of social institutions in accordance with what is believed to be God's Will, and by an evolutionary view of human history. This theology is to some extent implicit in their conception of the Church, though it should be added that other modern trends of thought have equally contributed to its development.

8. MODERNISM

Although there are very few Churches which would describe themselves as modernist, it is necessary to mention the modernist conception of the Church, because it has advocates in many Churches, and also because it raises important issues which should be taken seriously in any discussion concerning the nature of the Church.

The modernist conception is only "modern" because it has recently become an important theological tendency within Christianity; but its origins go back to individual thinkers of several centuries ago. At the same time there exists a relation between the more subjective conceptions of the Church formulated in the seventeenth and eighteenth centuries and the modernism of our day. For both emphasize the experiential rather than the "given" character of faith. The main *new* element in modernism is, however, the attempt to adapt Christian truth to the findings of science and to the contemporary secular philosophies. In so doing the modernist movement is convinced that it can appeal to the historical Jesus and to the Early Church, and that its conception of the Church is really a re-discovery of original Christianity.

It would be unjust to describe the modernist conception of the Church as the purely individualistic notion of an association of like-minded religious persons, or, as it was once put in the House of Commons in England, "a voluntary association for providing religious services on Sunday for that section of the population which chooses to take advantage of them." This notion is certainly widespread among the laity in many countries, but it has not been taught by the leading modernist theologians. Sometimes, however, more representative definitions of the Church come very near to it. Thus the well-known report, *Rethinking Missions*, rejects the Church "as a kind of magical institution, which confers certain mysterious gifts and graces upon its members, and which becomes an ark of safety for those who through it hope to secure thereby their eternal salvation in another world than this," in favour of the Church "as a spiritual fellowship and communion of those who have found a new spring of life and power by the impact of the Christian message, who are eager to join together as a living growing body of believers through whom the ideals and the spirit of Christ can be transmitted and His principles of life promoted."

In the statements of the leading modernist theologians one finds, however, a stronger emphasis on the transcendent and purely religious values in the historic conception of the Church. A good example is an article by Ernst Troeltsch.[1] Troeltsch rejects the purely individual notion, because the elevating and saving power which comes from Jesus implies a pattern of life which is not produced by individuals, but produces the individuals. Worship is not the sum of the subjective emotions of the worshippers, but the common turning to that life which is represented by Christ. He considers that the conception of the Church as a mere association of individuals fails to appreciate the centrality of grace in all ·Christian faith. To believe in the victory of the Church means to believe that that religious and moral power which finds expression in the Christian community is one of the forces which are destined to be ultimately victorious. On the other hand, everything which has to do with the Church as an institution founded by Christ Himself with a special ministry and guarantees, as an organization which canalizes the miraculous forces of the Incarnation, should be given up, even in its more refined form of a supernatural institution which is confined to preaching. The community of the spirit of Christ is the highest and most inward power of personal religion, and in so far destined to participate in the victory of the good. And Troeltsch concludes that we cannot know whether it will hold that position alone to all eternity.

[1] In the Encyclopedia *Die Religion in Geschichte und Gegenwart*, first edition.

The typical and important characteristics of this conception are that it denies the claim of the historic Churches, that they are based on the absolutely and uniquely true revelation of God, and that it considers the Church as *one* of the forces, though the highest, among the various spiritual and cultural forces which are working in the same general direction of the ultimate good. Troeltsch states clearly that it might be better not to use the word "Church" for this conception, because that word is so definitely linked to the classical idea of a body which represents the one and only way of salvation. Other modernists, however, use the old expressions, but give them a different connotation. Thus Professor Raven writes that the Church "is the fellowship of those who live in Christ, and by Him are incorporated into His body, that is the Church. No initiation except that of sharing in His sufferings can admit us to it; no sacrament save that of daily dying and rising again can sustain us in it; no priesthood but that of the Christ-possessed ministers to it; those that are led by the Spirit of God, be they Jew, Turk, infidel, or heretic, are within its membership; all mankind belong to it if having eyes they see, if their lives display the fruits of the Spirit, if they have love one towards another."[1]

It is evident that this conception is supremely tolerant in its oecumenical attitude, so long as it does not meet with authoritative and, as modernists would say, intolerant claims. It is, however, an open question whether this conception does not lead logically to a conception of community which is inter-religious rather than oecumenical.

In its attitude to the world, modernism may take very different forms. In so far as it is bound up with individualism and liberalism, it may lead to a purely defensive

[1] *Jesus and the Gospel of Love.*

attitude against those modern forces which would subordinate the individual to the collectivity. In so far as it is bound up with moral idealism, it may lead to a social concern which sponsors various humanitarian causes. It is a fact that modernist Christians have often put their more orthodox brethren to shame by the leadership which they have given in Christian, social, or international action.

CHAPTER II

THE CHURCHES IN HISTORY

THE purpose of this chapter is not to give a bird's-eye view of Church History, but rather to describe briefly the various forms of interaction between the Churches and their historical environment. This is necessary for the following reasons.

In the first place, it is impossible to understand a Church apart from its concrete setting. For a Church is not only what it claims to be according to its doctrine, but also what it actually says and does (and does not say and do) in relation to its environment. To say this is not to deny that the Church is more than a sociological grouping, but to affirm that the Church, like its Master, takes human form, and that we have this treasure in earthen vessels.

In the second place, there are a number of Churches which underwent such profound changes when they were transplanted from one part of the world to another, or when they entered into a different historical era, that they should be understood in the light of their present position rather than in the light of their original confessions. This is true, not only of the Churches in the United States of America, and of the Younger Churches, but also of several Churches in Europe.

In the third place, it is clear that the particular historical and geographical situation in which a Church finds itself will have a bearing on its attitude to the problems which will be discussed at the Oxford Conference. This is not said in order to encourage Conference delegates to approach these problems from the historical rather than from the theological angle. For it would be a disaster if at the Conference we were to speak as representatives of our particular cultural traditions rather than as Christians who are seeking to discover the eternal truth of God which is valid in all our different circumstances. But precisely in order to distinguish more sharply between that which is abiding and that which is transitory, that which belongs to the content of faith, and that which belongs to the changing patterns of history, or sociology, or geography, it is necessary to see clearly the particular situation in which each Church finds itself. Unfortunately we can do no more than indicate in the briefest manner what particular circumstances the various Churches have to face, and how their relationships with the world affect their thought about their message and mission. In order to condense the description as much as possible, it will be necessary to mention under each heading only a few of the typical problems which the Churches have to face in each particular area.

I. THE ROMAN CATHOLIC CHURCH AND ITS ENVIRONMENT

In describing the Churches in History we shall have to use the geographical rather than the confessional principle of division; for the historical situations differ according to cultural areas. But we must make an exception for the Roman Catholic Church, for it is the only Church which confronts the world as a whole rather than any particular part of it, and which has a centralized international organ for the spiritual, moral, and legal direction of its adherents.

A discussion of the relations between the Roman Catholic Church and its environment must take the mediaeval solution of that problem as its starting-point. For the unified culture of the period which found its climax in the thirteenth century remains the classical example of the synthesis between Catholic doctrine and civilization in general. The Church created a social order; but in the process the Church's conception of itself and of its task in the world was itself profoundly modified.

Ernst Troeltsch has shown how the extraordinarily subtle balance between Church and society, between supernature and nature, and between Christian doctrine and natural law, which is characteristic of the mediaeval situation, is the result of two sets of forces, namely, those of theology and of theory on the one hand, and those of social life and of practice on the other hand. The comprehensive system of Thomism is thus not only the formulation of the guiding ideals of mediaeval culture, but also the explanation and justification of a particular experiment in building a Christian order. The main features of this order are well known: the authority of the powerful and centralized ecclesiastical system over the whole of culture; the separation of the Church from the State, but not of the State from the Church; the adoption of a conception of natural law according to which the family, the authority of the State, the social order with its stratification in different stations, and with private property, all belong to the order of creation; the organic and patriarchal character of human relations; and the idea of the *Corpus Christianum*, the coterminous relation of Christendom and society, which—to use a phrase of Professor Ernest Barker—is "a single integrated community-State-and-Church."

This mediaeval pattern has remained the ideal of the Roman Catholic Church until this day. In fact, through the official sanction given to Thomism, it is to-day more than ever the normative conception of the Christian society. Thus the Encyclical *Ubi Arcano Dei* compares our present political anarchy with "that veritable League of Nations which existed in the Middle Ages, and which was a community of the Christian peoples," and Baron von Hügel considers the "Golden Age of Scholasticism" as "nearest to the ideal." It should, however, be added that there is a growing number of Roman Catholic theologians who consider that "the mediaeval dream has definitely come to an end, that the meaning of our revolutionary epoch is to do away with the last remnants of the so-called *Corpus Christianum*, and that in many respects the Church is thrown back into the situation of the early Church."

The peculiar character of the Roman Catholic attitude to society consists largely in this consistent loyalty to the guiding ideas of its classical epoch. Such new forces as those of capitalism and socialism, of democracy and totalitarianism, have not affected this attitude to any important extent; they have in fact only led the Church to organize itself more definitely for the defence of its heritage. The story of the Roman Catholic Church since the Council of Trent is essentially the story of the increasingly uncompromising and explicit definition of the ecclesiological and sociological ideas which were implied in the mediaeval order.

This, however, does not mean that the Roman Catholic Church is necessarily conservative and reactionary in its social and political attitude. For the application of the mediaeval principles leads in many cases to a progressive position in social questions. The famous Encyclicals on social questions have given a very vigorous denunciation of our present social and economic order, and contain far-reaching proposals for its improvement. Thus the Encyclical *Quadragesimo Anno* says: "Unbridled ambition for domination has succeeded the desire for gain; the whole economic life has become hard, cruel, and relentless in a ghastly measure." Roman Catholic politicians and sociologists have often been, and are to-day, among

the severest critics of capitalistic individualism; and
Roman Catholic trade unions and other societies have
played an important part in obtaining more advanced
social legislation. But official Roman Catholicism can
never accept such more radical solutions of the social
problem as those of Marxism, or even of democratic
Socialism, and that not merely because such movements
are often anti-religious or secular in character, but also
because the ideas of private property and of the limitation
of State interference in economic life are constitutive
elements of the Roman Catholic social ethic.

In practice, this means that Roman Catholicism as a
whole tends to defend those elements in society which are
still reminiscent of the corporative, pre-capitalist order,
and to oppose the movements of the social and political
left wing. Although it has no inherent sympathy with
nationalist and authoritarian movements, since they are
a constant menace to its universalism, and limit the freedom of the Church, it can make its peace more easily
with these than with the Communist movement, which
challenges the very foundations of the Roman Catholic
view of society. Seen in this light, the Concordats with
Italy and Germany, the attitude of the Vatican in Spain,
and the recent appeal to all Christendom to join in an
anti-Communist crusade, are logical consequences of the
general attitude of the Roman Catholic Church to society.
At the same time, Austria is an example of the positive
claims of the Church to permeate and guide the life of
the State, and of society as a whole.

The guiding conception is always that of the *Corpus
Christianum* under the leadership of the Pope. It is for that
reason that Roman Catholic jurists consider that the
Pope should act as arbiter in all international conflicts.
This is indeed a consistent claim for those who hold that
the Roman Church "is the most finished model of the

universal society, which disposes, through its organization
and institutions, of a marvellous influence to bring men
together, not only for the sake of their eternal salvation,
but even for their material prosperity."[1]

2. THE CHURCH IN ORTHODOX COUNTRIES

In order to understand the position of the Eastern Orthodox Church in relation to its national and social environment, it is necessary to remember that Eastern Orthodoxy
has gone through particularly tragic experiences, and that
it has practically never had an opportunity to express
itself in freedom. Again and again it has been confronted
with political forces which have tried to use it for their
own ends. It is only recently that sufficient autonomy has
been achieved to enable the Church, at least in some
countries, to elaborate its own answer *as a Church* to the
problems of the social order.

The Orthodox Church in its historical form is a child
of Byzantium, and until this day it shows the marks of
its origin. Justinian had declared: "Among the greatest
gifts of God bestowed by the kindness of heaven are the
priesthood and the imperial dignity. Of these, the former
serves things divine; the latter rules human affairs and
cares for them. And therefore nothing is so much a care
to the *Emperors* as the dignity of the priesthood," and had
thus laid the basis for a control of the Church by the
State. The Church accepted this situation, but not
without protesting again and again that "ecclesiastical
affairs are concerns of the priesthood and the theologians;
the administration of the exterior matters are the concern
of the emperor" (Theodore of the Studium). It is note-
worthy that several of the most highly-respected spiritual
leaders of Orthodoxy, such as John Chrysostom, John of

[1] Encyclical *Pacem, Dei munus pulcherrimum.*

Damascus, and Theodore of the Studium, opposed the totalitarian claims of the Emperors in order to gain freedom for the Church to proclaim its message without interference from the outside. Caesaropapism was, then, a condition imposed upon the Church rather than a condition desired by the Church. Charles Diehl, the specialist in Byzantine History, says: "Though in the age-long conflict between the Byzantine Church and the State, the Church was victorious with regard to the use of images, it did not succeed in overcoming the old tradition which gave the Emperor authority in religious matters."[1] It should be added, that the strong otherworldly tendency of Eastern Christianity often led to an acceptance of the world as it is, and to a recognition of a state and a society as Christian which "in a significant degree remained pagan, being only somewhat covered by the Christian garment."

The long period of Turkish domination in the Balkan peninsula, and the autocracy of the Russian Tsars, strengthened the tendency towards "the passive acceptance of, and even subjection to, all existing local governments, so typical for Orthodox Churches."[2] Orthodox thinkers have often justified this situation by attempts to give a doctrinal basis to the theory of Imperial theocracy, or of the religious significance of the Tsar, but voices have not been lacking which considered the interference of the State in religious matters as a violation of the freedom of the Church.

The result of this development has been that the Orthodox Churches are *national* Churches in the strongest sense of that term. Their life is bound up with the life of their nations to an extent unknown in any other part of the world. In the struggle to maintain national tradi-

[1] *Byzance, Grandeur et Décadence,* 1919.
[2] A. V. Kartashov in *The Church of God,* 1934.

tions during the Turkish domination, ecclesiastics were often the pioneers. The Oecumenical Patriarch acted as the political representative of the Christians in the Turkish Empire. In Russia, the identification of the Church with national aspirations was the result of another set of circumstances. The Church had been the great educator of the nation; and when the Byzantine empire collapsed Russia began to conceive it as its historical mission to become the "liberator of Eastern Orthodoxy, and of universal Christianity, from Mohammedan barbarism, and over against the Western heretics" (Dostoievski). This Messianic ideal of the "third Rome" and of the Russian people as the divinely-appointed representative of the only true faith has been a powerful element in Russian thought, and strengthened the bond between the Church and the nation.

The close connection between Church and nation is, however, not merely a matter of politics or of political ideology. It is at the same time the natural result of the Orthodox attitude to the world, which is based on the idea of the transfiguration of all earthly realities. The Orthodox Church is still in many places a "popular" Church, in the sense that it is near to the life of the ordinary people. This is especially true in the rural communities of Eastern Europe, which have not been affected by modern tendencies of thought.

In recent years, the situation of the Orthodox Church has been profoundly influenced by the new political and other currents of thought. In Russia the Church was first disestablished, and then persecuted. It is too early to say what attitude the Russian Church of the future, purified by its martyrdom, will take toward society; but it is likely that its attitude will be very different from that of the pre-revolutionary Church. However that may be, the year 1917 marks the end of the "Constantine period."

In other Orthodox countries the position of the Church is no longer so secure and unchallenged as it used to be, as secularism in one form or another makes headway. At the same time, Orthodoxy is in the midst of a process of reconsidering its relations to the world. There are many Orthodox theologians and laymen to-day who believe that the Church should be free and not serve a political régime, and who consider that "the days are coming to an end when the Church, as a loving teacher, protected and educated the submissive, or at least the docile energies of national life. It seems that a carefully-nurtured lamb can turn into a dangerous wolf, and has to be treated as such."[1] But other Orthodox leaders are still deeply convinced that only adherence to the old traditions of the closest possible relation between Church and State is truly Orthodox. To them the pattern of the Byzantine Empire, and of the developments which have grown out of it, is the normative ideal, just as the mediaeval pattern remains the ideal of the Roman Catholic Church.

In many different ways the Eastern Churches are giving evidence of their desire to use the greater freedom which they have gained for positive action in social and national life. There is increasing activity in such realms as education, rural work, and international understanding. And, what is even more significant, there is in modern Orthodox theology a movement towards a new explanation of Christian social doctrine which would "include all sides of the natural existence of man in the grace-abounding life of the Church." The interest which the Orthodox Churches show in the various oecumenical movements, and particularly in the "Life and Work" movement, is another sign of their present concern with questions of social morality.

It has sometimes been said that the Orthodox Churches

[1] A. V. Kartashov in *The Church of God*, 1934.

live in an "extra-historical" world. If that has been true in the past, it is no longer true to-day. One of the results of the historical crisis of our time, which has affected the Orthodox Church more than any other Church, is that the Orthodox Churches are consciously entering into history.

3. THE CHURCHES IN GREAT BRITAIN

In Great Britain, the relations between the Church, the community, and the State were for a long time dominated by the old assumption, inherited from the Middle Ages, that "in a Christian State or Kingdom one and the self-same people are the Church and the Commonwealth" (Hooker). This principle was at first applied only in favour of the Church of England, but since the attempts to impose Anglicanism on Scotland failed, its application resulted in the official recognition of two Churches each in a given territory, the Church of England in England, and the Church of Scotland in Scotland. Thus these two Churches became *national* Churches in that they claimed to embrace the whole community, and also *State Churches*, not in the sense that they were created by the State, but that they were Established Churches "secured and protected by the laws of the land." This does not mean, however, that these Churches accept the control of the State in spiritual matters. The Scottish Church has always been very emphatic on this point. When it declared in 1921: "This Church, as part of the Universal Church wherein the Lord Jesus Christ has appointed a government in the hands of Church office-bearers, receives from Him, its Divine King and Head, and from Him alone, the right and power subject to no civil authority to legislate, and to adjudicate finally in all matters of doctrine, worship, government, and discipline in the Church . . .",[1]

[1] Declaratory Articles.

it could affirm that these principles contained nothing which had not been claimed in the previous history of the Scottish Church.

In the Church of England the assertion of its independence from the State in spiritual matters was not made so categorically and consistently; but "the Church never abandoned its claim for spiritual independence."[1] Though the Church as such has not officially re-considered the question of its relations to the State until our own times, at different periods there have been powerful movements within it which have struggled for greater spiritual autonomy. The Non-Jurors, the Tractarians, the Christian Social Movement, and other forces have all contributed to the renascence of the principle that in matters spiritual the Church ought to be a self-determining and autonomous authority. The anomalous position created by the rejection of the Revised Prayer Book has recently provided another important element in the growth of this new conception. At the present time proposals are being studied which imply that the Church would remain a national Church, but that it would be free from the necessity of bringing measures related to spiritual concerns in any way under the control of Parliament.

For our present purpose the important point is that the Church of England has been increasingly affirming its spiritual existence as a Church apart from (and, if necessary, over against) the State and society. This development has its roots in a new understanding of the mission of the Church in the world. Although, in the past, the Church of England has often given the impression of being no more than the religious department of the State, and an organ of conservation rather than of prophetic leadership, under the influence of a deeper recognition of the implications of Churchmanship (the Oxford Movement

[1] *Report on Church and State*, 1935.

and the Evangelical Revival), and ot the Christian social task (Maurice, Kingsley, Westcott, the *Lux Mundi* group, and more recent Christian social movements), it has come to realize "the function of a national Church as the interpreter of the Christian creed, and the Christian code of morals, alike in the social and the economic spheres of citizenship."[1] The same may be said of the Church of Scotland.

In this respect, then, the Church of England and the Church of Scotland are to-day in a unique position. Both represent somehow the Christian faith of their nations as a whole, and both have the opportunity of speaking to the State and to the nation with an authority quite different from that of a free or disestablished Church-body. It is evident that this situation has its perils. For the close relation with the State may often lead to an uncritical identification with national interests. It should, however, be said that there have been many occasions on which these two Churches have expressed themselves very clearly and courageously. The report of the Archbishop's Committee on "Christianity and Industrial Problems" (1918), the action of Archbishop Davidson at the time of the General Strike (1926), and the resolution of the Lambeth Conference of 1930 on war (i.e. no support of a war in regard to which the Government has not declared its willingness to submit the matter in dispute to arbitration or conciliation), are instances which show that the Church of England "can no longer be counted on as a reliable bulwark of the existing social structure."[2] Similarly, a glance at the annual reports of the "Committee on Church and Nation" of the Church of Scotland will show that that Church conceives it as its duty to give Christian guidance to the nation as a whole in matters

[1] *Report on Church and State.*
[2] Maurice Reckitt, *Faith and Society*, 1932.

of social as well as of individual ethics, and that it does not merely echo the views of Government or nation.

The Free Churches—although their position is different, in that they do not seek to embrace the whole of the nation, and they have no problem of relations with the State,—have also developed a more positive attitude to their environment. Although their influence upon social and political life, more particularly in the vindication of freedom, has been great, they tended to become groups apart from the world, which thought of their task largely in terms of personal salvation and group sanctification. But more recently they have come to accept their share in the responsibility for the life of society as a whole. Though they were on the whole identified with Liberalism in politics, just as the Church of England was identified with political Conservatism, they have also provided leadership to various social and political movements which demand a more radical transformation of society. It is interesting to note that the majority of the older leaders in the Labour Party have come from the ranks of the Free Churches, and are still active Church members. This is, however, far from being true of the younger generation.

In spite of the many differences between the Churches, and groups within the Churches, the social doctrines of British Christianity appear to the outsider as a remarkably unified attitude. There are within the various Churches smaller movements of a more radical character, but the main current is that of a relatively optimistic and evolutionary view of social and international life. Thus the more eschatological position which conceives of the State as the God-given power to "restrain with the civil sword the stubborn and evildoers" (Thirty-nine Articles), has been generally abandoned in favour of a more idealistic conception, according to which the State has a positive value in the natural order, its true *raison d'être* being the purposes of men in co-operation, and not the use of force. The influence of the Catholic conceptions of the relations of nature and grace, and of the sacramental character of all life, has permeated many sections of British Christianity, whether they be nominally Catholic or nominally Protestant.

The most distinctive characteristic of the situation of the Churches in Great Britain is certainly that "the Churches are not dominant, but still all-pervasive," so that "even the most bitter political struggles fail to break the forms of a Christian culture."[1] In Britain, as elsewhere, the attempt is being made by many "to form a civilized, but non-Christian mentality"; but it has not taken such an aggressive form as in other countries. Thus British Christianity is not forced into opposition to its environment. This situation involves the danger of "official" Christianity, but it involves also the opportunity of influencing national life as a whole.

4. THE CHURCHES ON THE CONTINENT OF EUROPE

The Protestant Churches on the continent of Europe have also inherited the mediaeval ideal of the *Corpus Christianum*, and of the intimate connection between Church, Society, and State. In the sixteenth century "the conceptions of Church and State in the modern sense were still unknown; the basic idea was that of *Christendom*."[2] Both Luther and Calvin made this conception, in different ways, the basis of their views of the relations between Church, Community, and State. Thus Lutheranism in Germany accepted the principle "*cuius regio, illius religio*," which led to the formation of national (or terri-

[1] Reinhold Niebuhr in *The Christian Century*, November 4, 1936.
[2] Sohm, *Kirchenrecht* I, 1892.

torial) Churches, whose *"summus episcopus"* was the ruler of each particular territory. In Switzerland and in Holland, Calvinism established national Churches, which were more independent, but still closely connected with the respective Governments. Both Confessions demanded from the Government that it should protect the Church and resist heresy.

The great change which has come about in the position of the European Protestant Churches may be described in terms of the breaking up of this old unity of State, Society, and Church.

The *State* soon began to develop absolutist tendencies, and put the Church in a position very different from that which the Reformers had desired for it. Instead of fulfilling the demands of the Church, it claimed the right to interfere in Church life, and that not only in matters of constitution and discipline, but also in matters of faith and worship. In the eighteenth century it became the current conception among constitutional theorists that the exercise of religion should be not only supervised, but also controlled by the Government. This Erastian doctrine was a caricature of the ideas of the Reformers concerning the duties of the State toward the Church.[1] But the Church was not sufficiently alive to its dangers to resist the claims of the State. In the nineteenth and twentieth centuries the rise of liberal democratic states led in some countries to a separation between Church and State; but in these countries, as well as in countries where the Church remained "established," the State continued to restrict the sphere of action of the Church.

Society became less and less homogeneous, and more and more secularized, as the waves of the Enlightenment, of the French Revolution, and of Marxist socialism passed

[1] See Sasse, *Kirchenregiment und weltliche Obrigkeit*, Bekennende Kirche, Heft 30.

over Europe. The intellectual classes became largely indifferent to all religion, or turned to non-Christian philosophies. The working classes lost their confidence in the Church, because it was too closely bound up with the (capitalist) State, or because it did not show sufficient sympathy with the cause of social justice.

The *Church* was slow to realize that the *Corpus Christianum* ideal had become a fiction, that both State and Society were developing along their own lines without regard for the Church, and that European civilization was slowly disintegrating as the old common convictions lost their power in the community. Instead of asserting its spiritual autonomy, it accepted for a long time the supremacy of the State, and instead of making an aggressive evangelistic effort to win the masses back to Christianity, it lived on the strength of its tradition. Thus it became increasingly isolated and lost touch with the forces which were transforming social and cultural life. It was only towards the middle of the nineteenth century that the Churches in Europe slowly began to wake up to the new situation. Through various revivals, some of a more pietistic, some of a more ecclesiastical character, and some in the realm of social action, the Protestant Churches again became participants in the spiritual conflict.

But since secularism had become the dominant element in European culture, the action of the Church took the form of defence rather than of attack. Liberal, socialist, and more recently totalitarian parties and governments, tried to eliminate the influence of Christianity in the fields of politics, social service, and education, and were to a large extent successful in doing so, because Church members were not alive to their responsibilities. The first task of the various revival movements was therefore to strengthen Church consciousness, and to organize the

Christian forces. The Calvinist revivals in Holland (Groen van Prinsterer and Kuyper) and in Hungary; the Lutheran revival in the Church of Sweden (Manfred Björkquist and Einar Billing); and the Inner Mission in Denmark, are examples of this development.

Some of these new movements, however, did not confine themselves to the strengthening of the Church. Although their theological positions were very different, the Dutch Protestant parties, the religious socialists in Switzerland and other countries, the Christian social movement in Germany, the collaborators of the Sigtuna foundation in Sweden, and the *"Christianisme social"* in France, all desired to make Christianity once more a force for righteousness in social and political life.

In the post-war years there has been a rediscovery of the Reformation which has expressed itself in many different ways; although it has strengthened the confessional consciousness, it is a unified movement, to this extent, at least: that it demands a clear recognition of the uniqueness of the Christian message over against the various secular philosophies of our time, and seeks to re-capture the spiritual autonomy of the Church.

In Germany the conflict between the Church and the modern world has taken a particularly acute form. Though there had been a number of movements which had tried to revive a consciousness of the spiritual independence and of the evangelistic and social task of the Church, the Church as such was too divided and too closely connected with the old tradition of territorial Church government to undertake the responsibilities imposed on it by the spiritual situation of the country. The disestablishment of the Churches after the World War did not produce a decisive change; and so the Church as such was unprepared for the completely new situation which arose in 1933 when the National Socialist

party came into power. On the other hand, the
theological renewal which had taken place in the ten
years preceding 1933 had prepared the way for a new
and deeper understanding of the nature and function of
the Church, so that there was far more spiritual substance
in the Church than appeared on the surface. This is not
the place to describe the Church conflict in Germany;
but it should at least be noted that the issue with which
the German Church has to deal is not simply the old one
of the right relations with a more or less Christian or
indifferent Government, but rather of the relations with
a movement which is consciously based on a particular
semi-religious ideology, and determined to have its
ideology accepted by the nation as a whole. The issue is
complicated by the fact that a section of the Church
advocates a synthesis between Christianity and National
Socialism, and claims that the Church's faith and order
should be adapted to the new ideology. In the face of
these attacks on the very basis of the Church's existence
there has arisen a strong movement of "confessing"
Christians, who resist all attempts to introduce into the
Church ideas concerning faith or order which do not have
their origin in Holy Scripture and the Confessions. Thus
there is in Germany to-day an *ecclesia militans* which is
struggling hard for the right of the Church *to be itself*, that
is, to speak and act in obedience to Jesus Christ, and to
Him alone.

The Church conflict in Germany is not an isolated
phenomenon, but, rather, a striking example of the general
conflict which has arisen between the Church and European civilization. In many countries the Church is confronted with the problem of its attitude to the powerful
new political ideologies, which are all more or less
totalitarian, and therefore attempt to use the Church for
secular ends. The European Churches are thus forced to

a realization of the fact that the era in which Europe was officially Christian is over. "The elements (i.e. the Gospel and the world) which had rightly or wrongly become combined, are being separated. Thus the Church is called to a completely new freedom in its witness to, and its understanding of, the Gospel. Not to an escape from the world or out of the world, but to a freedom in the world such as did not exist in the order inaugurated by Constantine. Not to a freedom from its solidarity with the world, and therefore not to a freedom from its mission, its responsibility, its service in the world, but to a freedom to fulfil its own mission, to accept its own responsibility, and to render its own service *in* the world and *for* the world."[1]

At the present moment the Churches in Europe are in the midst of the difficult process of learning this lesson. In so far as they are alive to the signs of the times, they realize that, in the face of new conceptions of state and of society, they must reconsider their traditional ideas concerning the relations between the Church and the world. It is therefore practically impossible to generalize about the convictions of the European Protestant Churches in relation to the State and the Community. Large sections of European Protestantism are still unaware of the new challenge; others try to get the Church to identify itself with anti-communist and pro-capitalist, or anti-fascist and pro-socialist "fronts," and still others have come to see that the task of the Church is not to allow itself to be exploited for secular purposes, but to combat all ideologies which make totalitarian demands, and to proclaim its own message of concrete obedience to the claims of Christ. The newer theological development which is now beginning to affect Church life as a whole, and particularly the younger generation, leads to a critical evaluation of

[1] Karl Barth in *Theologische Existenz Heute*, No. 25.

the various entangling alliances between the Church and the world, to a healthy impatience with the bourgeois conservatism which is still widespread in Church circles, and to attempts, chaotic as yet, but none the less encouraging, to elaborate a Christian ethic in relation to modern realities. It is unlikely that these attempts will lead to a crystallization of thought and attitude until the great preliminary issues of the nature of the Church and its message have been faced so radically and so generally that the Church can once more speak with spiritual authority.

5. THE CHURCHES IN THE UNITED STATES OF AMERICA

With very few exceptions the Churches in the United States of America owe their origin to the history of the Church in Europe. But this does not mean that they can be understood in the light of their European antecedents. On the contrary, the peculiar conditions of American history have shaped the life of these Churches to such an extent that it can be said that in the United States of America "the Church entered on a new development."

The distinctive characteristics of the situation may be summarized in the following three points: (1) If we take the United States of America as a whole, no Church can claim to be predominant, either by virtue of numbers, or by virtue of its connection with national history; there are at least eight groups of Churches, each of which can claim to have played a large part in the spiritual history of the country. (2) The Churches whose origins go back to what Troeltsch has called the "sect type" (voluntary societies rather than mass Churches), represent about two-thirds of American Protestantism. These Churches have therefore been able to become the dominant force in the religious situation. (3) Although in the early period of

American history there were a number of "established" Churches, none of these was ever established in relation to the nation as a whole. The first amendment to the Constitution said clearly that "Congress shall make no law respecting an establishment of religion," and though this meant at the time simply that the states were left free in matters of religion, it led inevitably to a separation between Church and State. It is important to remember that "the reason for writing the amendment into the basic law of the land was no hostility or indifference to religion, but rather an unwillingness to curtail the freedom of the states in religious matters, or to give federal support to any particular form of Christianity."[1]

The effects of these circumstances upon the conception of the Church have been momentous. The great variety of existing Churches, and the absence of any comprehensive national Church, meant in practice that Christians in the United States began to think in terms of *Churches* rather than of *the Church*. This tendency was strengthened by the influence of the "sect type," which emphasized the local congregation rather than the common national or international bond. It is interesting to compare the conviction of John Robinson, the Congregationalist pioneer, that the word "Catholic" defined the nature of the Church rather than its extension, and that the only reality was the particular Christian organization, with the following statement in a recent report to the Federal Council: "To an extraordinary degree the loyalties of our membership are concentrated on the local church. There is a declining measure of loyalty to the denomination. There is very little sense of loyalty to the Church as a universal order of human life."[2]

The separation of Church and State worked in the same direction. For it meant that the Churches became volun-

[1] S. McCrea Cavert.　　　　[2] *Report on The State of the Church.*

tary societies in the eyes of the civil law. "Inevitably this idea has strongly affected the thinking of Church people about the Church. It is directly encouraged by their legal status, and flourishes in a democratic atmosphere."[1] The report which has just been cited says: "Many Churches are depending too largely to-day upon the same motives which maintain clubs, lodges, and philanthropies." The extraordinary frequency of changes from membership in one denomination to membership in another, confirms the truth of this observation.

Thus the Churches in the United States are characterized by a far greater mobility than the Churches in Europe. Theirs is a "spirit of innovation" (which was, of course, specially strong on the frontier) leading to a "divorce from the historic past." "Not since the first three centuries, with their many branches of Gnostics, has the Church anywhere seen so large a body of Christians who have broken so nearly completely from much that is normally termed the Catholic tradition."[2] More recently, however, there has grown up, especially among the ministry, a new interest in Catholic theology and Catholic forms of worship.

In their relation to society, the Churches in the United States have tended to become increasingly "organizations concerning themselves largely with the establishment of the Kingdom of God on earth."[3] They belong to the "theocratic" type, which "deals with the problem of realizing God's Will," which has "not so much the character of a carrying and including mother, as that of a ruling and commanding father," and in which "the holy is sought, not given, for it is dependent on decision and perfection."[4] The Puritan ideal led them to feel

[1] Robert Hastings Nichols.   [2] K. S. Latourette.
[3] Robert Hastings Nichols.
[4] Paul Tillich in *Social Research*, February 1936.

responsible for the moral welfare of the nation; and so (with very few exceptions) the Churches have constantly tried, and often with success, to influence the social morality of the nation as a whole. Since the beginning of this century the "social gospel," which has found many followers among the ministry, but which has affected the laity to a lesser extent, has been seeking to widen the ethical concern of the Church to include the whole of society. Thus many Churches have gone on record as favouring far-reaching adjustments in the social order. And the Federal Council of the Churches has worked out a "Social Creed" based on its purpose "to transform society in accordance with Christian ethical ideals," and has spoken out on a large number of specific social issues.

On the other hand, the desire to be in the closest possible touch with the life of society and of the nation, and the gradual disappearance of the eschatological emphasis of the older Puritanism, and of the exclusivism of the original "sect" ideal, have led to a blurring of the distinction between the Church and the world. "The dividing line between Church and Society becomes indistinguishable. . . . As a consequence there has never been a really life-and-death struggle between religion and secularism in America."[1] Thus the Church has often become so much a part of secular society that it could not effectively challenge it. Moreover, its danger, like that of most European Churches, is that it should become identified with one particular class. The report on "the State of the Church" says: "Another entanglement of the Church to-day which impresses us as a matter of grave concern is its assimilation of the assumptions and ideals of the comfortable middle class."

In different ways the Churches in the United States are to-day engaged in the attempt to recapture the prophetic

[1] Reinhold Niebuhr in *The Christian Century*, November 4, 1936.

element in their Christian tradition, and to become once again Churches which are in the world, but not of the world. The critical analysis of the present situation in the report on "the State of the Church" leads up to the conclusion that "the Christian Church needs to disentangle itself from various forms and habits of mind characteristic of our present society, that it may take hold of the moral and spiritual issues of that society with greater sincerity and power." This same note is predominant in the theology of many younger theologians, and leads to a reconsideration of the older forms of liberalism and "Social Gospel" theology. There is no desire to give up the concern for society as a whole, but it is believed that the basis of a critique of society is a transcendent loyalty, and a new conception of the suprahistorical character of the Church.

The problem of the relations between Church and State is once more being widely discussed. Though it cannot be said that the American State has totalitarian tendencies at present, there have been signs which show that the possibility of a development in the totalitarian direction is a real one, and that the question of the relations between Church and State is by no means solved. The situation has been summarized by Samuel McCrea Cavert in the following terms: "In several European countries to-day the burning question for the Church is —how can it maintain its own freedom against encroachment by the State? In America the question is—how can the Church influence and guide the life of society and the State? Unless we can answer the American question now, we may have to face the European question later."[1]

---

[1] For a full treatment of the problem of Church and State in America see *Church and State in Contemporary America* by W. Adams Brown, New York, 1936, which has been written with special reference to the Oxford Conference.

6. THE YOUNGER CHURCHES

The Younger Churches differ greatly from each other in the realms of doctrine, forms of worship, and Church order, for they reflect the many differences which exist between the Older Churches to which they owe their origins. But they have much in common in the realm with which we are dealing in this section, for they are all confronted by civilizations which are based upon and conditioned by non-Christian religions. In Asia as well as in Africa, "Christianity comprises only a small minority of the people; and although its influences radiate far beyond this immediate circle, it is a new and foreign phenomenon in a world of deep-rooted religions, ancient institutions, and customs. The Younger Churches are beginning their career in face of changes as gigantic as any that have taken place in history. . . . The meeting between Europe, the most vital power of recent centuries, and the East has caused a psychological, social, cultural, moral and religious earthquake in the East. . . . It is within this general framework that the meeting between Christianity and other religions takes place. . . . The small Christian communities have to fulfil their task and develop their life amidst a world in transition, a transition in which they are themselves involved."[1]

The most difficult aspect of this situation is certainly the fact that, owing to the simultaneous appearance in Asia and Africa of Western political penetration and Western Christian missions, in the eyes of Asiatics and Africans Christianity is a part of, and an expression of, Western expansion. This misunderstanding has often been strengthened by the impression created by certain missionary methods, which seemed to be aiming at creating Churches on a purely Western rather than on

[1] H. Kraemer.

an Eastern or African model. Again, the fact that the overwhelming majority of members of the Younger Churches have come from classes of the population which had little or no share in the cultural life of their nations, has imposed great handicaps on the Church in relation to its environment, and has often made it appear to be an exotic institution.

The main task which faces the Younger Churches is therefore that of becoming truly indigenous to the various nations in which they live and work. All over the East "the indigenous Church is a problem, not a fact,"[1] though some Younger Churches are more advanced than others along this line. The main issue is not merely whether the Younger Churches can become fully self-governing and self-supporting, but rather whether these Churches, after having become independent, can find such a relation to their cultural, social, and political environment that their message is not misunderstood as denationalizing propaganda, but understood as a supranational and eternal gospel. There is also, of course, the danger that the attempt to relate the Church to its environment may lead to an adaptation of the *content* of the Christian message to non-Christian systems, and thus to a syncretism which is spiritually powerless. The situation is further complicated by the fact that the Eastern mind tends to regard the traditions of the collective group as the authoritative norm in all matters of faith and morality, and does not distinguish clearly between national cultural heritage and religious truth.

The Younger Churches are attempting to deal with these problems by emphasizing in word and act their solidarity with their national environment, while remaining loyal to the common heritage of the Christian Church. Thus, there are many signs that in theology and worship,

[1] D. T. Niles in *The Student World*, Fourth Quarter, 1935.

in religious art and literature, they are seeking to express themselves less and less in Western, and more and more in Eastern forms. Again, several of the Younger Churches have come to support the national political aspirations of their people. "Perhaps the most interesting development of recent years is the fact that Christianity, which was once upon a time so aloof from the thought and life of the people, has capitulated, and come to an understanding with nationalism."[1] In most of the countries concerned this nationalism is a nationalism of self-expression rather than of conquest or domination. But the relations to the national movements remain a delicate problem, for every form of nationalism may develop into a new religion which crowds out loyalty to God. "The Younger Churches are thus exposed to the severe test whether they can be so open to the moving of the Spirit of God as to be able to discern where their solidarity with the national ideals demands whole-hearted service of the nation, and where their fundamental solidarity in God demands prophetic utterance amidst, and, it may often be, against their own people."[2]

The relations between the Younger Churches and the State vary considerably, because the States with which they have to deal are so different. In India and in the Dutch East Indies, the Governments take an attitude of prudent neutrality towards all religions. They do not help the Churches in any way, but neither do they hinder their development, except in so far as they create the impression that they prefer the religious *status quo* to any large-scale conversion movements. In China the Government is not unsympathetic to Christianity, but has forbidden the teaching of religion in registered private schools. In Turkey, all forms of religious propaganda are

[1] S. K. Datta in *The Student World*, Fourth Quarter, 1930.
[2] H. Kraemer.

forbidden. In Japan, the State is proclaiming its own religious absoluteness with increasing definiteness and exclusiveness, and demanding from adherents of all religions that they should take part in Emperor-Worship, which is called a merely patriotic cult, but which has in fact the characteristics of religious worship. The Younger Churches are thus beginning to be confronted with the same issues which have arisen in several Western countries; but the difference is that they have neither numbers nor a Christian tradition behind them.

In their attitude to the social order, the Younger Churches have given their main attention to the practical tasks of rural reconstruction, mass education, and the improvement of industrial conditions. These tasks are so pressing, and so overwhelming, that the more theoretical problems of social ethics have necessarily been given a secondary place. In Japan and China, however, the emergence of communism has led to the formation of movements which advocate changes based on Christian principles in the social order. There is, for instance, the well-known movement of Toyohiko Kagawa, which considers the co-operative movement, in its various forms, to be the Christian solution of the social problem. But other Christians in the Far East, and more recently in India, incline towards more radical solutions along the lines of the socialist parties of the West.

It is obvious that the peculiar conditions in which the Younger Churches find themselves will also have a great influence on their conception of the Church. But since the Younger Churches are still in the process of formation, it is too early to say what this influence will be. There is a danger that impatience with the Church-as-it-is, combined with the individualistic tendency of much missionary teaching, may lead to a "Churchless Christianity." On the other hand, there is genuine desire for Church unity, which has found expression in the actual union of various Churches in China and India. The declaration of the National Christian Conference at Shanghai in 1922: "We believe profoundly that only an united Church can save China," certainly represents the convictions of many leaders of the Younger Churches. But in this matter much will also depend on the attitude of the Western Churches. "It is an open question whether it is going to be possible to go forward with plans for unity in the Eastern countries and in Africa, unless the crucial questions are faced in the Western Churches with the same keen desire to overcome them."[1]

[1] William Paton. For a full treatment of the problems with which the Younger Churches are confronted, see Mr. Paton's recent book, *Christianity in the Eastern Conflicts*, which has been written with special reference to the topics to be discussed at the Oxford Conference.

CHAPTER III

THE CHURCH AS AN OECUMENICAL SOCIETY

1. IS THERE A CHURCH IN THE CHURCHES?

OUR survey of the various doctrinal conceptions of the Church, and of the position of the Churches in the world, leaves an impression of bewildering variety and lack of unity. It is, of course, true that an attempt to state the peculiar characteristics of each Church leads automatically to an over-emphasis on the points of difference and disagreement, and that there are many cases in which there is far more actual agreement between the Churches than their official utterances would seem to indicate. The Churches do not exist in isolation, but influence each other in numerous ways. And historical situations arise in which Churches of differing confessional backgrounds may be brought very near to one another. On the other hand, it must be admitted that there are also examples of the opposite development. Agreement in formulated conceptions does not necessarily mean fundamental and lasting agreement. There are Churches which are characterized by much inward conflict in spite of the fact that they possess generally-accepted standards of faith.

The fact of variety remains, then, a basic reality with which we have to deal. But it is not the only reality. The survey of the conceptions of the Church shows that there are certain important points upon which all those Churches which are taking part in the oecumenical movement are agreed. The chief of these seem to be the following :—

1. All consider that the Church is not merely a human

organization, but a community of which Jesus Christ is the Lord, and in which He is at work. In other words, all conceive of the Church as an object of *faith*.

2. All agree that there is essentially only *one* Church, since there is only one Lord. As a reality of faith, the word Church has no plural.

3. All agree that the Church in which they believe is not exhaustively expressed in any given Church body.

The importance of these points should not be underestimated. That the Churches connected with the "Life and Work" movement hold these common convictions about the nature of the Church means at least that they have a common point of reference. If they disagree, it is about the nature of one and the same thing, and not, as would be inevitable on a more inclusive basis, about a series of completely different things. It is only on the basis of a clear understanding that the Church is essentially different from any other religious or moral institution that the Oxford Conference can hope to find common answers relevant to the issues which have to be faced. And it is essential that in the utterance of the Conference and in the life of the oecumenical movement this common understanding should find clear and unequivocal expression.

But while these points of agreement are important, they do not lead us very far. For as soon as we try to implement these statements, and take them as the basis for common speech or action, we find that they bear different meanings according to the confessional background of the person who uses them. We agree that Jesus Christ is the Lord of the Church; but to some this means that His Lordship is a Lordship which does not admit the introduction into the message of the Church of any other authorities, such as tradition or natural law; to others it means, on the contrary, that tradition, in which they see the continuing life of Christ in the Church, and the orders of nature, in which they see the revelation of God's continuous working, are equally authoritative. Similarly, if it is said that there is only one Church, this implies for some Churches that only one visible Church is the true Church, but for others that no visible Church can claim to be *the* Church of Christ, since all Christian Churches together represent that reality. These examples might be multiplied *ad infinitum*; but the point is clear, namely, that our belief in the Church is both the basis which enables us to meet together, and at the same time the barrier which makes us unable to speak with a united voice.

It may be asked whether it is not possible to avoid this difficulty by leaving this issue aside, and by attempting to find agreement on Christian ethics irrespective of doctrine and ecclesiology. In a sense, that is what the Stockholm Conference of 1925 attempted to do. Its committee meeting at Hälsingborg in 1922 stated in a letter to the Secretary of the Lausanne Conference Committee that its desire was to see Christians act corporately "as if they were one body in a visible community," for "this can be done by all equally without calling theological principles in question" (*ohne dass theologische Prinzipien angefochten werden*), and "doctrine separates, but service unites."[1] But the experience of the subsequent development of the oecumenical movement has shown that this position needs qualification. At Stockholm it was already becoming clear that no lasting understanding in the realm of ethics can be arrived at, unless there is some measure of understanding concerning the assumptions which underlie all ethics. The presupposition that there is a fundamental unity between Christians in question of ethics

[1] Nathan Söderblom, *Pater Max Pribilla und die Oekumenische Erweckung*, 1931.

proved to be an over-simplification of the real situation. As we have seen in our discussion of the relation of the Churches to their environment, the differences which exist in that realm are quite as considerable as the differences in the purely doctrinal realm. The need for a theological clarification became even more clear as the Stockholm movement found itself confronted with secular philosophies whose significance consisted precisely in the fact that they advocated, not merely a different morality, but a wholly different outlook upon life, which challenged Christianity at its very foundation. At the same time, it was increasingly felt that a body representing the Churches would never be able to speak with any spiritual authority if it were to continue to eliminate from its discussions the basic question of the nature and the function of the Church. And so it has become inevitable that, as Dr. Oldham puts it, one of the questions of fundamental importance which are at the heart of the discussions on Church, Community and State, should be: "What is the nature and mission of the Church?"

It may further be asked whether the Oxford Conference should not at least deal with the question of the Church from a purely objective and neutral standpoint. If that means that the Conference should not choose one of the many different conceptions of the Church as the only true one, this question should, of course, be answered affirmatively. But if it means that the Oxford Conference should try to speak from a standpoint above and beyond the actual standpoints of the participating Churches, the question should be answered negatively. For a standpoint which transcends the actual standpoints of the Churches does not exist. It might perhaps be constructed; but in that case the Oxford Conference would create a new and different Church, and no one will seriously maintain that that is its function. The difficult reality is that there is no "oecumenical" conception of the Church which can be accepted by all the Churches or even by a large majority. The very essence of the oecumenical problem is precisely that the Churches are not at one on this basic matter, and that no Church, in itself, can claim to represent the solution of the oecumenical problem. It is a *conditio sine qua non* of any oecumenical work that each Church, and the oecumenical movement as a whole, should realize this fact, and not try to cover it up by ambiguous language which means different things to different people. It is only by a frank facing of real differences that advance can be made in the realm of Christian co-operation and unity.

There is a theory of oecumenical relationships which solves the difficulty of the relations of the Churches to *the* Church by looking upon the existing Churches as branches of the one true Church. According to this theory, no Church by itself is *the* Church, but each Church is part of *the* Church, and the purpose of the oecumenical movement is to express the spiritual wealth, the variety, and the symphonic harmony which are inherent in Christendom as a whole.

This view of the oecumenical situation has its partial justification in the New Testament image of the relation between the Body and its members. There is a sense in which the various Churches need each other, in order to be corrected by each other, and in order to express more adequately the fullness which is in Jesus Christ. But the branch theory generally means more than this, and stands for a conception of tolerance which owes its origins, not to the Bible, but to modern humanitarianism. Its weakness is that it isolates the question of *unity* from the question of *truth*. We have seen that the various conceptions of the Church do not merely supplement one another (although they do that to some extent), but they also contradict one another. It is difficult, for instance, to speak of harmony when some Churches say: "The revelation of God is transmitted through the Holy Scriptures and the Holy Tradition,"[1] and other Churches say: "Jesus Christ as witnessed unto in the Scriptures is the one Word of God. We reject the false teaching that the Church should acknowledge other events and powers, systems or truths in addition to and besides this one Word of God as source of its proclamation and as revelation of God."[2] Although it should not be forgotten that these two statements are in so far incomparable that they have been formulated in very dissimilar situations, it is clear that they represent conceptions of the Church which differ fundamentally from each other. In other words, the reality of the situation demands that everyone must choose between the existing doctrines, or (which amounts to the same thing) choose against all of them in favour of a new and different conception. The branch theory finally denies the validity of those conceptions of the Church which claim to be *true*, and not merely to be aspects of a many-sided spiritual harmony. And this is in fact what all Churches claim, and must claim, though they claim it in different ways and in relation to different doctrines. At any rate, the advocates of the branch theory must recognize that in the oecumenical realm their view of the Church is just one among many others, and that it cannot claim to be *the* oecumenical theory.

It is precisely because we have to do with nothing less than the Church which is the Body of Christ that we dare not think in terms of opportunism or compromises. The reasons why we should bury our divisions, and present

[1] Statement agreed upon by the delegations of the Anglican and Rumanian Churches at Bucarest, 1935.
[2] Declaration of the Confessional Synod of the German Evangelical Church at Barmen, 1934.

a truly united front to the world, are indeed pressing and weighty. No one who has thought through the issues which will be discussed at the Oxford Conference can fail to feel this, and feel it deeply. We should therefore always ask ourselves: Are our differences really of such importance that we dare not give them up? And we should not have the slightest hesitation in doing so; in fact, we are obliged to do so, if we can do so without sacrificing our loyalty to Christ. But we are no less forced to ask the other question: Can we give up the truth for which our Church stands without becoming disloyal to *the* Church, that is, to the truth which Christ Himself has revealed to us? For it is the duty of each Church to care desperately for the truth of God; if it ceases to do so, it ceases to be a Church with a message of God, and becomes simply a philosophical institution which has no longer a message of salvation for men or for the world.

The position is, then, that we believe together that there is a Church in the Churches, but that we cannot say together how and where it exists, or how and where it functions. For some, the marks of the Church are the traditional ones of acceptance of the creeds and the episcopal order; for others, they are in the exclusively Biblical purity of doctrine; for others, in the personal faith of the Church's membership; for others again, in complete freedom of doctrine and worship. It is therefore, humanly speaking, impossible to discover how out of these different approaches we may come to one common conviction as to what the Church in the Churches really is, and how it should be concretely expressed in oecumenical form.

There is no "way out" of this situation. For every so-called "way out" proves in fact to be an element which complicates the situation even more. We are therefore obliged to recognize the fact of our disagreement as to the *nature* of the Church as well as the fact of our *agreement* as to the *reality* of the Church. This means, not that we should cease to work for unity, but that we should cease to try to force the issue of unity. Our present *impasse* is a sign that unity cannot be made by men, but can only be acknowledged and received when God actually gives it. It is with unity as with all the gifts of God: we can prepare for it, we can pray for it, we can watch for it, but we cannot bring it into being. Unity is not achieved; but it *happens* when men listen together to God, and when He is willing to give it to them.

In the meantime, the Church in the Churches, or better, the Church Universal, remains a reality in which we *believe*. As such, it is the great critical principle in the life of all Churches. The very great value of the oecumenical movement consists in the fact that by its very existence it reminds us of the challenge of that criticism. In its light we see more clearly how much our Churches have become entangled with the world of nations and races and classes, and how little they have lived up to their faith in the Church Universal. In its light also we discover what elements in our divisions are no more than very relative cultural or other human idiosyncrasies which have no right to hold the Churches apart. In its light we become troubled in our consciences about the self-satisfaction and complacency of our Churches, and learn to pray that God may give us the unity which we ourselves are unable to realize.

2. CAN THE CHURCHES SPEAK AND ACT TOGETHER?

At first sight it seems quite superfluous to ask whether the Churches can speak and act together; for ever since the Stockholm Conference the Churches have been co-operating through the Universal Christian Council for Life and Work and other oecumenical bodies. But in the light of our survey of the conceptions of the Church and of the oecumenical situation, the question arises: What does this co-operation mean? Does it mean that the Church in the Churches has in fact found its embodiment, in spite of the doctrinal and ecclesiastical barriers between the Churches? Or is this co-operation simply a question of machinery which has nothing to do with the Church-as-such? It is important to face these questions; for it is evident that our view of the significance and character of the Oxford Conference, as well as of the work of the Universal Christian Council, will largely depend on the answers given to them.

The kind of oecumenical activity of which the Oxford Conference is an expression can be conceived in two ways. It is possible to conceive of it as a process of study, research and discussion, the purpose of which is to help individual Churches and individual Christians to fulfil their Christian duty in relation to the world, but not to speak in any sense as representing the Church of Christ. There is much to be said for this position. It is first of all a modest position, which does not arouse expectations which it is hard to meet. The Churches have indeed much to learn from each other, and a pooling of Christian thought concerning the present world situation, and the Christian task in that situation, is so useful and timely that this purpose alone seems a quite sufficient justification for the holding of a World Meeting. Another advantage of this view would seem to be that it is based on a realistic acceptance of the fact that at the present moment no oecumenical conference can claim to speak officially for the Churches or to legislate for them.

But does this conception truly represent the actual situation; and does it do justice to the demands which are rightly being made upon the oecumenical movement? There are two reasons why it seems inadequate:—

In the first place, the Oxford Conference is composed of representatives appointed by the Christian Churches. And Churches are not like governments or scientific societies, which can meet without committing themselves. Churches are bodies which exist to proclaim the truth of God; and it is therefore their function, when they meet individually or together, to bear witness to the message which has been entrusted to them. Representatives of Churches can never meet without at least attempting to live up to their main obligation, which is *to be the Church*, and to announce the Lordship of Jesus Christ over the world.

In the second place, the particular *purpose* of the Oxford Conference demands that, in addition to devoting itself to study and research, the Conference should be ready, if God wills, to speak on behalf of the *Ekklesia Theou*. This purpose is to give guidance to men and women in a world which has lost its way, and which is frantically trying to meet its problems with pagan or semi-pagan philosophies and principles. What this world needs to-day is not in the first place new ideas or theories, but the message of divine authority which the Church alone can bring, and the demonstration of the reality of the Church. Over against false conceptions of state and community, the Church needs to affirm the existence of a God-given community which transcends all human divisions, and that *as a reality*, and not merely as an ideal. This implies that the Conference, if it is at all to meet the opportunity and challenge of the hour, is obliged to affirm that it is itself an expression of that community.

It must, however, be admitted that this second conception of the oecumenical movement and of the Oxford Conference seems to raise as many questions as it solves. For, as we have already seen, it is impossible to maintain that the Churches which will take part in the Oxford

Conference have a common conception of the Church; and it is out of the question to claim that the utterances of the Oxford Conference will have official ecclesiastical authority, or that the Conference is at all comparable with a veritable Oecumenical Council.

But is it really the case that the Conference must be either a purely non-committal body of Church leaders, which registers agreements and disagreements, or a fully-authorized and representative body, which speaks officially in the name of the Churches? It would seem that there is a third possibility, which is harder to define, but which is nevertheless as real as the other two. This third conception is based on a recognition of the two basic facts in the oecumenical situation: the fact that all the Churches concerned believe in the Church as a reality which transcends any given historical Church body and is brought into existence, not by men, but by God; and the other fact that these same Churches cannot at present be brought together into one united Church.

It is impossible for the Oxford Conference to claim that its voice is the voice of the Church; but it is equally impossible for it to *deny* that it is such a voice. The *positive claim* is impossible because it can be made only when the Churches are ready to be re-united into one body in which all members accept each other as full members of the Church, and in which there is a basic agreement on the faith and order of the Church. The *denial* is impossible, because it would deny in advance that at the Oxford Conference (where more than two or three will be gathered in the name of Christ) Christ Himself may be present, and that the Oxford Conference may illustrate the truth: *Ubi Christus, ibi ecclesia*.

In these circumstances, the right attitude for the Conference to take is to leave open the question whether and how it represents the Church, but at the same time to be ready to be used as the Church of God, if God wants to use the Conference in such a way. Concretely, this means that the Conference should not only register points of agreement and disagreement, but also affirm the basic message of the Christian Church to the world, and thus show that it is concerned, not merely with trends of thought, with theories and conceptions, but above all with the witness to the reality of the Kingdom of God which has come to the world in Jesus Christ. Thus the Conference would not only speak *about* the Church, but (*Deo volente*) would manifest the living actuality of the Church, and its relevance to the world.

If the Conference were to think of itself in this way, its authority would reside, not in official prerogatives or the power to represent and commit individual Churches, but simply in the truth of whatever it has to say. Orthodox and Catholics and Protestants can meet on this ground. They may disagree as to how the truth which they seek together in the Biblical Revelation is finally distinguished and recognized, some using as their criterion the acceptance of truth by the Church as a whole (*Sobornost*, or the principle of *quod semper, quod ubique, quod ab omnibus creditum est*), and others putting their confidence in the inward testimony of the Holy Spirit; but they can agree that in some way which we cannot exactly define, the Church of Christ may speak through the Oxford Conference.

It is obvious that the Oxford Conference, so conceived, would in no way become a substitute for a truly united Church. For a united Church would be characterized by a great deal more than this. It would speak on the basis of substantial agreement in essentials, while Oxford can at best speak only in spite of fundamental disagreements. Only a united Church would be able to give a fully adequate demonstration of the meaning of the

Church, as in it there would be the full fellowship of witness and of sacraments in common.

It is possible that the oecumenical movement in the present situation may be little more than an international humanitarian organization. It is also possible that, though it is not the Church of Christ in its fullness, it may be an "earnest" of the Church of Christ which is in the Churches, and is more than the Churches. Whether the Oxford Conference will represent the first or the second of these two possibilities we cannot know in advance. But in prayer and work we can prepare ourselves to be used as the Church, and to give a common witness, in order that the world may know that Jesus Christ has been sent by God.

PART III

THE FUNCTION OF THE CHURCH IN SOCIETY

by

Dr. J. H. OLDHAM

CHAPTER IV

THE PREDICAMENT OF THE CHURCH

BEFORE we proceed further in our inquiry it is well that we should pause for a moment to reflect on the conclusion reached in the last chapter that the Churches, while disagreeing in regard to the nature of the Church, are at one in believing in its reality, and that they all hold that the Church is not merely a human organization but a community of which Jesus Christ is the living Lord. Familiarity must not blind us to the pivotal and startling nature of this assertion. On its truth all discussions of the function of the Church in society hinge. It would be, on the other hand, a disastrous self-deception to ignore the fact that for the great majority of men to-day the faith which the Churches confess is incredible, or at least irrelevant to the problems with which in actual life they have to deal.

It has been the conviction of the Church from the beginning that it owes its being to an act of God in history. It is the abiding witness to the manifestation in history of a new reality. The Christian faith is not merely that events which took place in Palestine nineteen centuries ago have been the source of spiritual influences which have had a profound effect on the life of mankind. That is an indubitable historical fact. But the Christian faith expressed in the doctrines of the Incarnation and the Atonement means more than this. It implies that events took place which changed fundamentally the relations between God and man and instituted a new era in human life. History now possesses a centre.[1] From

---

[1] Cf. Tillich, *Religiöse Verwirklichung*, pp. 110–17 (of which an English translation appears in his *Interpretation of History*, pp. 242–65), and his paper in the forthcoming volume on *The Kingdom of God and History*.

this centre it derives its ultimate meaning. This belief has determined men's reckoning of time. Our chronology divides history into the period which preceded and that which follows the birth of Christ.

The first Christians lived in the consciousness that a new age had dawned. As a leading modern scholar has recently said, "the New Testament writers are clear that history is henceforward qualitatively different from what it was before Christ's coming."[1] God had sent forth his Son that men might receive the adoption of sons. Of this new reality the Church is the witness and the continuing embodiment.

The significance of the Christian assertion that history has a decisive centre is especially apparent to-day when men in large numbers are becoming dissatisfied with an "unchartered freedom" and the relativity of their own choices and are turning passionately to an absolute that can command their unquestioning loyalty. Many are finding this reality outside themselves to which they can make a complete surrender in the objective facts of race and nation. To men who are seeking for a truth outside themselves to which they can give their lives, it must make all the difference whether that to which the Church points them is a world of ideals or a world of solid and inescapable fact. Christianity has always claimed to point men to the latter. Its message has been that a new day has dawned, that the Word became flesh, that the grace of God has appeared, bringing salvation to all men. It speaks in the indicative, not the imperative mood. Religion, as Baron von Hügel continually insisted, begins and ends with the *given*.

The question of the content of the Christian faith and of the nature of the Church lies outside the scope of the Oxford Conference. Its programme has to do with the

[1] C. H. Dodd, *The Apostolic Preaching*, p. 217.

relation of the Church, as it exists in the world to-day, to the community and to the State. But at every point these fundamental issues are involved. We cannot address ourselves to the real situation in the world to-day if we put them out of our mind in order to get on with the job of applying Christianity to the social needs and tasks of our time. The important question for the world as well as for the Church is what is the Christianity which we want to apply. The real crisis of the Church relates not to its social programme but to its faith. The two are not unconnected. But to embark inconsiderately on a discussion of the first without a deep awareness of its dependence on the second would be to play with a grave situation.

We cannot hide from ourselves that the truths to which the Church bears witness in its historic creeds, the central affirmations of its testimony, have for multitudes in what has been known as Christendom become unreal and meaningless. They seem to accord neither with the growth of knowledge nor with men's actual experience of life. As an English critic has put it, modern unbelief results from a widespread conviction that "the creeds of the Churches cannot command a total act of the whole moral being."[1]

The problem is not, of course, new. The position of the Church has always been one of predicament. It has from the beginning made its appeal to what is best in men, and been at the same time a scandal. The gospel of Christ crucified has never at any time been other than a stumbling-block and foolishness. The situation in which we now find ourselves, moreover, is the result of a process which has been going on for centuries. Ever since the Renaissance Christian thought has struggled to come to terms with the new and growing knowledge and the

[1] Hugh Fausset, *The Modern Dilemma*, p. 19.

changes it has brought about in men's outlook and the conditions of their lives. But the question has been raised sharply by recent movements in theology, and is pressed home on us still more searchingly by the grave situation in which we find ourselves, whether, in the acuteness of the struggle, the substance of the Christian faith has not in many instances been surrendered. It is a necessary task to interpret the Christian faith to the mind of each age. But it is no less necessary to be sure that what we are restating is the Christian faith and not something else, or merely some fragment of it. The plight of the world is too serious to allow us through loose thinking to substitute for the beliefs which have sustained, nourished and inspired the lives of Christian men and women through the centuries some totally different religion. This is not the place to inquire how far particular theologies, ancient or modern, conserve or discard the essentials of the Christian faith. It must be clearly in our minds, however, that all discussions relating to Church, community, and State turn on the central question whether the affirmations which have formed the core of Christian conviction through the centuries still have significance for the world to-day. If these affirmations have ceased to be valid, it is not easy to see why the Church should be regarded as having crucial significance for the life of the world. If it has nothing to say to men beyond what they can by reflection on their own experience discover for themselves, if it does nothing more than add a religious flavour to the values which the community is already pursuing, the salt surely has lost its savour, and the significance of the Church for society becomes of secondary importance. The Church may, perhaps, be worth preserving as a cultural association. But unless it has a Word that is not from men but from God, a Word of divine redemption, a truth not of its own making to which it can point men, it is not the Church in which through the ages Christian men and women have found salvation and power to serve the world.

It would be a dangerously false diagnosis, however, and a complete misunderstanding of the situation which must engage our attention to suppose that all that is needed is a return to orthodoxy. The problem is far more complicated. A complacent return to orthodox theology would be an evasion, not a solution, of the problem of the Church in the world to-day. If that were all, the effect would be to reduce Christianity to an esoteric faith of a relatively small, and probably diminishing, number of the faithful, lacking any real relevance for the total life of the world. It would be to renounce the mission of the Church to the world as a whole, which is implied in the faith that it is the bearer of a divine revelation and redemption. For the cardinal fact with which we have to reckon, when we propose to take the Church seriously, is that for large sections of the population in what was formerly known as Christendom—not to speak here of the non-Christian world and its needs—the traditional Christian ideas have ceased to have any living meaning. It is not so much that men disbelieve in Christianity as that they feel it to be entirely irrelevant to their actual experience of life. It may be doubted whether Christian people as a whole are alive to the extent to which this loss of meaning has taken place. Those whose responsibilities, as clergy or Church workers, compel them to move for the most part in circles over which the Christian tradition retains its hold, have often little idea how completely unintelligible what is said in the pulpit is to the large classes of which we are speaking—unintelligible in the sense that it makes no effective contact with their experience. There is, of course, a preaching which makes itself intelligible by saying nothing very different from what the listeners already know and think. But the problem which concerns us here is that of giving to the tremendous and startling affirmations of the historic Christian faith a meaning and expression which makes a living challenge to the thought and life of the ordinary man.

Only by a firm resolve to be rid of all shams and make-believe and to face unflinchingly the truth, however unpalatable, can the Church hope to become an effective force in the world to-day. Let us, therefore, on the threshold of our present task attempt to see without illusion the position of the Church in the present life of the world.

If the picture is not to get out of perspective, we must remember that general statements do not apply in equal degree to all countries; and we must also give full weight to the remarkable advances of Christianity in the past two centuries. This period has witnessed in the modern missionary movement the widest expansion of the Christian faith that has taken place in Christian history. The Church has followed up the vast migrations of European peoples to North America, Australasia, and South Africa and succeeded in maintaining the allegiance of these new nations to the faith of their forefathers. Professor Paul Douglass in his paper in the forthcoming volume on *Church and Community* has drawn attention to the fact that whereas at the close of the American colonial period probably not more than 5 per cent of the population belonged actively to the Church, the proportion is now 50 per cent, and in the twentieth century the ratio of Church members to the total population is higher than it has ever been before in the history of the American Churches. During the past century and a half, as Professor Latourette has pointed out in a contribution to the same volume, more new orders and congregations have come into existence in the Roman Catholic Church than in the whole of its previous history. Similarly, there have been in Protestantism many new movements within the Churches and many new enterprises undertaken by them, and such widespread organizations as the Young Men's Christian Association, the Young Women's Christian Association, the World's Student Christian Federation and the Sunday School Movement have come into existence. Far-reaching movements for humanitarian reform, too numerous to mention, have drawn inspiration and support from the Churches or have had as their promoters and leaders men and women impelled by the Christian motive.

It would be wrong not to draw from these facts encouragement and hope for the future. But they must not blind us to the fact that there has gone on simultaneously during the same period throughout the world an immense secularization of men's thoughts and interests. The work of the world is carried on without serious account being taken of the Christian affirmations, which, if they are true, transform all our ideas about the meaning and end of man's existence, about his relations with his fellows in society and about the ends of his economic and political activities. It is, perhaps, a reason for encouragement that in some countries to-day the persecution of the Church is making the profession of the Christian faith in a new sense a live issue.

Take the modern universities in Europe and America and Asia, where the youth of the world are acquiring their ideas about the ends and tasks and responsibilities of life. In how many will you find among the members of the teaching staff more than a very small minority of convinced Christians? The tide in some quarters is perhaps turning. It has been said with some truth that in certain countries in Western Europe, while the masses are drifting away from the Church the intellectuals are beginning to return to the faith. In French literature at the present day the claims of Christianity are a subject of keen debate. But it remains none the less true that in the universities of the world the problems of man and of society are being continuously studied without heed being paid to the central Christian affirmations as an interpretation of life that merits serious consideration.

Or, again, visit any of the large cities in countries traditionally and professedly Christian and ask among those who bear the major civic responsibility and who are conducting the activities of social welfare, including those who still retain the habit of attendance at the services of the Church, for how many of them the historic assertions of the Christian faith are a living, conscious inspiration; or, as a still more illuminating question, for how many these affirmations constitute the substance of a clearly held faith which they desire and endeavour to transmit to their children. The number will probably be found to be very small. Or, consider the multitudes among the working classes in all western countries which have broken consciously, and to all appearances irrevocably, with the Christian tradition because its assumptions and values have no recognizable relevance to the realities of their lives. Between their whole way of regarding life and what is uttered in the pulpit there is a gulf which in many instances seems to be unbridgeable.

Add to this that in Russia, and perhaps increasingly in other parts of the world every agency for moulding and influencing public opinion is being used deliberately and with concentrated energy to implant in the minds of the whole population conceptions of life totally irreconcilable with the Christian view so that the capacity even to understand the latter may be almost wholly destroyed.

It is not suggested that the Church alone is to blame for this state of things. Our purpose is not to criticize or assign responsibility but simply to see the facts as they are. The secularization of life is the result of men's choices. They have given themselves to the pursuit of this-worldly ends. They have preferred the material to the spiritual. They have sought the heaven upon earth which they believed that their own efforts could enable them to create. They are captivated by utopias which hold out the promise of comfort and prosperity. They live by theories which blind them to the realities of human existence. They are no longer able to see the ultimate facts which encompass man's life—the realities of death, sin, judgment, and God. This concentration of interest on the present life, which is ultimately rooted in the choice of individuals, passes into and permeates the whole texture of social life so that it becomes the climate and temper of the age, to the benumbing influence of which all, Christians as well as non-Christians, are in greater or less degree subject. There is a prevailing insensibility to spiritual issues which causes the message of the Church to fall on deaf ears.

But while the responsibility for this state of things does not lie wholly with the Church, its failure and short-coming have contributed to the result. It has not swum with sufficient vigour against the stream. It has allowed its own life and attitudes and activities to become secularized. If it is to serve the world it must begin with an inward reformation. Its consideration of its relations to society and the State must be rooted in a deep repentance.

What is demanded of the Church in this situation will engage our attention in the pages which follow. But in order that we may approach our task with fitting humility it is well that we should recognize at the start that the

Churches represent only a minority, and, if we disregard
those whose adherence to Christianity has ceased to be
more than nominal, only a small minority of the population of the world. Even where the Church still appears
to be a considerable factor in the life of the community,
we must be on our guard lest the historic position of the
Church, the force of persisting custom, the impressive-
ness of a large enrolled membership and the tolerant
and friendly indifference of the community and of the
State conceal from us an inner weakness and loss of
power to give real direction to the thoughts and purposes
of men. The judgment of one of the keenest observers
of the contemporary scene may almost certainly be taken
as not merely an individual opinion, but as expressing
the mind of many thoughtful laymen who stand outside
or on the fringe of Church life. "Protestant Christianity,"
writes Professor A. N. Whitehead, "so far as concerns
the institutional and dogmatic forms in which it flourished
for three hundred years as derived from Luther, Calvin,
and the Anglican Settlement, is showing all the signs of
a steady decay. Its dogmas no longer dominate: its
divisions no longer interest: its institutions no longer
direct the patterns of life."[1] The Churches will accomplish their purposes in proportion as they are free from
illusions regarding the ability of the Church to mould
the economic, political, and international life of our time.
The frank acknowledgement of our own weakness and
impotence will drive us back on the true and unchanging
source of the strength and hope of the Church. It is in
the power of God to enable the Church now and in the
coming days to utter a word which will not be without
effect on the life and conduct of Christians, and will not
be unheard even by a secularized, indifferent, and hostile
world.

[1] *Adventures of Ideas*, p. 205.

CHAPTER V

THE CHURCH:

SOME NECESSARY DISTINCTIONS

NOTHING has done more to confuse the discussion of the function of the Church in society and of its relation to social and political issues than the habitual use of the general term Church to cover a variety of quite different meanings.

It is not necessary to refer again to the theological differences in the understanding of the Church, to which our attention has already been directed. These must be in our minds throughout the discussion. Our purpose in this chapter is to focus attention on three distinctions of the highest importance in relation to the rest of our inquiry.

I. THE CHURCH OF FAITH AND THE CHURCH AS INSTITUTION

We want, first, to call to mind, without committing ourselves to any particular theological interpretation of the facts, a distinction which in some form is recognized by all Churches. The Church as it exists empirically has a double aspect. It is, on the one hand, the body of Christ, composed of those who are united to Him by a living faith and a loyal and active discipleship; and it finds its embodiment, on the other hand, in a divine-human society, organized for the purposes of worship, teaching, mutual edification and service, and drawing into its membership from a variety of motives many whose adherence is largely formal and carries with it no commitment to the obligations of the Christian life. The distinction which Troeltsch made between the "Church" type and the "sect" type is familiar. The emphasis of the Church type is on the Gospel as something objectively given which exists prior to any act or decision of the individual and is embodied in the life of an institution, and on the universality of the Gospel; of the sect type on the act of personal faith and decision of the individual. But the distinction on which we wish to insist here is one that applies to what according to the definition of Troeltsch are sects as well as to Churches. Most of the bodies which began as sects, i.e. as companies of professed believers with strict internal discipline and standards sharply differentiated from the world, have come with their growth in numbers to include many nominal and indifferent members and have relaxed their tension with the world. Dr. Paul Douglass, in the paper already referred to, writes that to-day "the American Church is obviously no longer a collection of sects separated from, and at war with, society. Indeed it has become a segment of society quite like the rest. Still less in the persons of its individual members is it a collection of saints, that is of individuals inwardly distinguishable from the mass by a unique faith or by the peculiar graces of Christian character."

Where a national Church has come to include a number of persons whose adherence is purely nominal and whose membership carries no sense of obligation, or where a society professing the Christian name becomes little more than "a quasi-religious and quasi-cultural enterprise, which is frequently content to add a pious phrase to whatever values, cultural, social, and political, the community may be pursuing,"[1] it has ceased to bear, in this inclusive sense, any kind of resemblance to the Church of the New Testament. All existing Churches are in greater or less degree mixed bodies. They cannot exclude from member-

[1] Reinhold Niebuhr in *The Christian Century* of November 4, 1936.

ship those who are in need of instruction, education, help, and healing. There is an inescapable tension between the holiness of the Church and the universality of its mission and ministry. The Church is not an invisible community of elect spirits. It has an actual existence in history, and is real only in its actual historical embodiments. But we cannot attribute to these mixed bodies the characteristics of the true Church of Christ, or expect from them in their corporate capacity the action which can rightly be demanded from those who have committed themselves whole-heartedly to Christian discipleship. We dare not overlook the fact that the Church as an organized society may become perverted and corrupt, so as to deny in its life and practice the faith which it professes and to be changed into the very opposite of what it claims to be. We can never forget the unceasing tension between the divine and the human elements in the Church. To call that Church which is not Church and to include in our thought of the Church what is in reality a denial of the truth of Christ is an impiety. From the tension of which we have spoken there is no escape. The Church cannot cease to be an institution, nor can it limit the universality of its ministries. Within the Church as an organized society the true Church has to be continually re-created, and to find new embodiment in the faith and obedience and devotion of those who hear and respond to the voice of Christ.

2. THE WORSHIPPING CONGREGATION AND LIFE IN THE WORLD

A second distinction of fundamental importance is that between the Church as a society organized for the purposes of worship and teaching and the life of Christians in the world. It is the paradox of religion that it is at one and the same time concerned with the whole of life and has

also its specific and distinctive forms of expression, obligations, and responsibilities. It is, on the one hand, a
surrender of the whole life with all its activities to doing the
will of God; and it finds expression, on the other hand, in
a conscious and deliberate turning of the mind to Him in
prayer, thanksgiving, and meditation. It is a fundamental
weakness in the present relation of the Church to society
that we have allowed our conception of the Church to be
determined almost entirely by the second of these two sides
of the Christian life.

The difficulty has its roots in the fact that the
Church as an organized society is distinguished from
other forms of human association by its concern with
worship and teaching. As we shall see in a later chapter,
these are not simply particular forms of human activity,
but acts constituting the being of the Church. But it is
disastrous if the truth that the ministry of the Word and
the administration of the Sacraments constitute the
Church, and that it is the performance of these acts that
differentiates it from other human activities, leads us to
suppose that worship is the whole or characteristic business
of the Church. The Church is a worshipping community.
But it is at the same time a company of redeemed persons
transplanted into a new sphere of life in which their
actions are determined by new principles. The God whom
the Church worships is a God who has a will and purpose
for the world. The business of the Church is to do His
will, and the place where it has to be done is in the world.
It is a business not only for Sundays, but for weekdays.
The Church as an organized society is not an end in
itself, though we are always tending in practice, if not in
theory, to make it an end in itself. It exists for the sake of
the world, and it is fulfilling the purpose of its existence
in the measure that through its worship it is alive and
operative in the world.

In relation to the issues which will come before the Oxford Conference nothing could be plainer than that if the Christian faith is in the present and future to bring about changes, as it has done in the past, in the thought, habits, and practices of society, it can only do this through being the living, working faith of multitudes of lay men and women conducting the ordinary affairs of life. The only way in which it can affect business or politics is by shaping the convictions and determining the actions of those engaged in business and politics. It remains inoperative and unproductive except in so far as it becomes a principle of action in the lives of those who are actually carrying on the work of the world and ordering its course in one direction or another. Obvious as this truth is, and certain as it is to receive assent when stated, it does not, in fact, fill any large place in the picture called up in our minds when we use the word Church. The word does not in the least suggest the work of the world. It suggests Sunday, and what happens on Sunday. We can hardly exaggerate the loss resulting from this restriction of meaning.

One result of the limitation in our thought of the term to the Church as organized for purposes of worship and teaching, and to the other activities undertaken by the Church thus organized, is that when we discuss the witness and action of the Church in relation to society our minds run at once to action by ecclesiastical assemblies or by the clergy. We do not stop to think that incomparably more important than either of these in its effect on the life of society is what ordinary Christian people are doing day by day in the working week. To take but one illustration, every modern State has a vast and expanding system of social services. In the operation of these services there must be hundreds, or thousands, or tens of thousands of Christian men and women. What they can accomplish for social betterment in the ordinary fulfilment of their daily tasks must far outweigh anything that can be undertaken by organized Church agencies. But we do not think of the former work as having anything to do with the Church. It has somehow come about that an immense fund of Christian action and witness has lost association with the idea of the Church.

Religion has come to be thought of as one department among others instead of something that is concerned with the whole of life. To the man in the street religion is one of the many special pursuits followed by people who have a bent in that direction. A false dichotomy dominates the whole of our present thinking and colours our ordinary speech. We refer, for example, to prayer and worship as entering into the presence of God—as though God were not present in every moment of our lives and in every action we perform. "To go into the Church" is a phrase that is often used to describe a vocation to the Christian ministry. When we speak of the Church fulfilling this or that function in the social sphere we tend instinctively to think of the clergy doing something about it or of assemblies, in which the clergy predominate or take the leading part, taking some action. To a far greater extent than we ordinarily realize our whole thought about the Church has become clericalized. If the Church is to be an effective force in the social and political sphere our first task is to laicize our thought about it. We stand before a great historic task—the task of restoring the lost unity between worship and work.

3. DIFFERENCES OF FORMS OF ACTION

There is a third distinction which is very seldom made in discussions of the relation of the Church to society, but which is essential for any profitable consideration of the subject. The failure to make it clearly and decisively has been one of the principal hindrances in the way of a true and fruitful understanding of the functions of the Church in the social and political spheres. It is the distinction between the persons, or classes of persons, by whom any proposed action is to be taken. Action is always action by persons, acting individually or collectively. In regard to any intended action, therefore, it is always necessary to ask by what persons it is intended to be carried out. Lack of clearness on this point means evasion of responsibility. Action by the Church may in practice mean several entirely distinct things. It may mean action imposed or recommended by the authorities of the Church. It may on the other hand be intended to refer primarily to action by the clergy. Or, again, the action intended may mean action by the Christian laity, either in the faithful discharge of the general duties of their vocations as Christians, or in and by a particular association formed for the achievement of specific social and political ends, the pursuit of which they believe to be demanded by loyalty to the Christian profession. All these forms of action are quite different from one another, and failure to distinguish between them, and the unreflective use of a general term "Church" to cover wholly distinct forms of action, has been the cause of an immense amount of confusion about the function of the Church in society. We fail to distinguish the question of what Christians can do from the quite different question of what the Church as a society organized for the purpose of worship and teaching can or ought to do. We limit our possibilities by thinking of them in terms of a body in which the leadership and initiative are largely in the hands of the clergy, instead of in terms of the activities of the Christian men and women who are engaged in the practical affairs of the world.

If it could be secured that in the future no one should ever demand or recommend that the "Church" should do something without defining what concrete steps he has in view, and on whose shoulders in particular the responsibility for what is proposed is to be laid, a far-reaching service would have been rendered to the Christian cause.

CHAPTER VI

THE CHURCH AND THE WORLD

OUR understanding of the function of the Church in society and of its relation to the Community and the State depends in the last resort on our doctrine, or our undefined and unconscious assumptions, regarding the relation of the Church to the world.

The preparatory work for the Oxford Conference has brought forth such a variety of divergent and conflicting views on all the subjects that have been studied that it is difficult to find one's way through the maze. It may help in some degree to clarify the issues if an attempt is made to distinguish some of the major differences of view on the subject of the relation of the Church and the world which have manifested themselves in Christian history and still to-day divide Christians into opposing camps. A full and satisfying treatment of the questions with which this chapter deals would require the labour of many years and a wealth of knowledge to which the writers can make no claim. In the selection of the material and in the treatment we have been guided in the main by the questions which have forced themselves to the front in the preparatory work for the Oxford Conference. We can do little more than point to important issues to which Christian thought must be directed with increasing vigour and determination in the years to come. But without some preliminary understanding of these issues, and the differences in the understanding of them, the Church cannot come to grips with its real tasks. Discussions about the relations of Church, community, and State will remain on the surface of things, and those who take part in the debate will find themselves at cross purposes with one another.

No scheme of classification can be entirely satisfactory, especially when limitations of space permit of only the most cursory treatment. The views here distinguished for purposes of thought are not mutually exclusive. The lines frequently cross, and on particular issues there are often groupings which cut across the main divisions. A fuller and more detailed exposition would disclose many strange bedfellows, and on certain questions the representatives of a particular tradition are sometimes found in surprising company.

We shall set down the different views side by side in order that they may mutually criticize one another. Our purpose is not to decide which interpretation and attitude is right, but to see in each the truth after which it is striving and to recognize at the same time those elements of incompleteness or weakness which prevent other Christians from giving it their assent. The differences which the survey will bring out are so great and deep that the first impression may well be that no basis of agreement can be found and that there is little possibility even of mutual understanding. Historical controversy has often driven the upholders of a particular view to adopt an absolutist position and to sharpen the opposition to an extent which prevents them from recognizing any elements of truth in the view they are combating. There is a strong probability, however, that any view which has won the assent of Christian minds has some root in Christian experience and attempts to express some element in Christian truth, and that, up to a point at least, even the sharpest divergences spring from the desire to emphasize different aspects of a reality too rich and many-sided to be comprehended in any single interpretation. And even if, on some crucial issues, the opposing convictions seem not so much to supplement as flatly to contradict one another and to confront us with the responsibility of clear decision between two irreconcileable alternatives, we may still, perhaps, gain from the view which we reject some corrective of a too narrow interpretation of that to which we commit ourselves. If we are prepared to listen with patience to those views which most arouse our antagonism, and to try to understand them, we may find that the conceptions which we find least congenial have much to contribute to the enlargement of our understanding of spiritual realities.

The questions we shall consider in this chapter are not, as some may think, theological abstractions of interest only to professional theologians. They are involved in every practical question with which the Church to-day has to deal. We have only to let our minds dwell for a moment on the history of the Church during the past nearly two thousand years to realize that the question of the relation of the Church and the world leads us straight to the springs of Christian action. The various attempts to answer this question have moulded the whole history of the Western world. The gigantic struggle between the Papacy and the Empire which dominated the Middle Ages, affected the lives of generations of men and has left its traces on subsequent European history, hinged on the question of the relation of the Church to the world. The flight from the world of the Christian mystics, and the attitude of the Christian groups, which in all periods of Christian history, have laid the whole emphasis on individual salvation, offer another solution of the problem. The Reformers of the sixteenth century, in their vehement repudiation of the solution of the Middle Ages, claimed to be restoring the Biblical conception of the relation between the Church and the world. The historical developments to which this claim gave rise, which took different forms in countries under the influence of Lutheranism and Calvinism respectively, are too well known to call for mention. In our own day the social and political doctrines embodied in the papal encyclicals, the social gospel which seeks to provide a Christian solution for all the needs and problems of society, the Barthian theology which utters an emphatic protest against any confusion of the gospel with social aspirations and Utopias, are each rooted in a particular understanding of the relation of the Church and the world. It is this same issue, moreover, which is at stake in the struggle between Christian faith and the new religions which claim to know the real needs of human society and desire, for the achievement of their own purposes, to absorb or to suppress Christianity.

I. THE BIBLICAL VIEW

Before we consider the different views of the relation of the Church to the world which have emerged in Christian history, we may recall to our minds the essential features of the Biblical attitude to the world. The attitude of the Bible is expressed in three main convictions, which differentiate it from that of all other systems of religion or philosophy.

In the first place the world is God's creation. God is the Lord both of nature and of history. As created by God the world is good. It is God's world, to be received and enjoyed as His gift. "To us there is one God, the Father, of whom are all things." Every creature of God is good. "Every good gift and every perfect boon is from above." There is in the New Testament no trace of the dualism which depreciates the material in contrast with the spiritual.

Secondly, the world is corrupted by sin. Hence men need to be saved *from* the world. The world has its dangers for the soul. Its attractions and interests draw men's hearts away from the love of God, which is the supreme good. Christ bade his followers not to lay up treasure on earth but in heaven. Christians are warned not to love the world nor the things that are in the world; to set their minds on the things that are above, not on the things that are upon the earth; to use the world as not abusing it. They are strangers and pilgrims on the earth. To gain the whole world cannot make up for the loss of one's own soul.

The world is not only something which may be over-valued. It is dominated by the forces of evil and is in definite opposition to God's Kingdom. It hates Christ and His followers. It lies in the evil one. The friendship of the world is enmity against God. Thus the attitude of Christians to the world is one of acute opposition. The Cross of Christ is a condemnation of the values of the world. Through it the world has been crucified to the Christian and he to the world. Christians are baptized into Christ's death in order that they may walk in new-ness of life. They are called to mortify their members which are on earth; to put away the old man and put on the new. They are not to be fashioned according to this world, for the fashion or scheme of this world is passing away. In the world Christians must expect to have tribulation. Christ sends His disciples as sheep in the midst of wolves.

Thirdly, God's purpose is to save the world. It is the object of His redeeming love. Hence the Church has a mission to the world. As Christ was sent by the Father into the world, so He sends His disciples. They are to be the light of the world, the salt of the earth. They are ambassadors on behalf of Christ, beseeching men to be reconciled to God, who, in Christ, was reconciling the world unto Himself. They are not to be overcome of evil but to overcome evil with good. The ultimate victory is assured. For Christ has already overcome the world. The Church is a rock against which the gates of hell cannot prevail, the body of Christ which fulfils His sufferings, fights His battles, and shares His victories. The Christian can declare that he is "more than conqueror." This note of hope and assurance is characteristic of the whole New Testament. It is not based on confidence in personal achievements, but on the invincibility of God's purpose of redemption. "Whatsoever is begotten of God overcometh the world; and this is the victory that hath overcome the world, even our faith."

In these fundamental convictions the problem of the relation of the Church to the world has its origin and source. They give rise to a tension which can never be fully resolved in this earthly life. The world has to be both denied and possessed. In Christianity both world-affirmation and world-denial are raised to the greatest heights. There is for Christians the thrill of those who have entered into the liberty of the sons of God, and who know that all things are theirs and that all things work together for good to them that love God. On the other hand, for the sake of the Kingdom of God they are called to sacrifice all that they most prize, including, if need be, life itself.

2. NATURE AND SUPERNATURE

The most massive, coherent, and fully worked out attempt in Christian history to find a solution of the relation between the Church and the world is that embodied in the system of Thomas Aquinas. Through its influence on the whole life and activities of the Roman Catholic Church, of whose attitude it still remains the acknowledged and dominant interpretation, it possesses a historical significance which can hardly be overestimated.

In modified forms its fundamental conceptions have exerted a powerful influence in other Churches also, and have in many subtle and indirect ways affected the general Christian attitude towards the world. We must be content to indicate a few of the main features of this view of the world, without taking account of the existence of other tendencies of thought within the Roman Catholic Church or following out the variations of these leading ideas which find expression in other Churches.

M. Etienne Gilson, in his Gifford Lectures on *The Spirit of Mediaeval Philosophy*, has a chapter on "Christian Optimism" as a fundamental characteristic of the Catholic attitude to the world. The unshakable foundation of this optimism, as it finds expression in the Fathers and in the thinkers of the Middle Ages, is the first chapter of Genesis, in which it is declared that God created the world, and that because He created it, it is good. In spite of the state of fallen nature the world still declares the glory of its Creator. There is indeed no Christianity without the hatred of the world, *contemptus saeculi*, but hatred of the world is not the same thing as hatred of being. On the contrary it is hatred of not being.[1]

This statement gives expression to the fundamental conviction of Catholicism about the relation of the Church and the world. Both are manifestations of the eternal being of God, though they manifest that being in different degrees. The problem of the right relations between the Church and the world is thus ultimately a problem of ontology. The fact that the concrete problems of the social and ethical life are to be interpreted in the last resort in terms of a metaphysic of being is of decisive importance for the traditional Catholic attitude to the world.

The world has its place in a firmly fixed and unalterable

[1] *L'Esprit de la Philosophie Médiévale*, pp. 111–32.

hierarchy of being, which has its source and culminating reality in God. In this created world God has implanted the law of His own being. This eternal law of God embraces the whole universe and controls the entire course of historical life. This is not, however, to conceive of the world in a static and unhistorical sense as lacking in life and movement. It is one of the central assertions of the Thomist philosophy that the created world is in ascending movement towards the Good. All life has a purpose towards which it strives. All these several purposes are directed to the final goal of participation in the perfect and inexpressible glory and majesty of God.

This massive endeavour to arrive at a clear and unified interpretation of the world is not, however, monistic. If it were it would be a denial of the essential Christian convictions of the radical nature of evil and of man's need of redemption and would no longer be a Christian interpretation of reality. The ontological continuity throughout the whole world, which consists in a universal participation in the eternal law of God, is a gradual one. Between the perfect being of God and the not-being of evil there are innumerable degrees of reality. It is this conviction that underlies the Thomist distinction between nature and supernature—a distinction which is central for its whole interpretation of the Church and its relation to the world, determining to a large extent the social and political attitudes of the Roman Catholic Church.

It would be wholly wrong to suppose that this interpretation of the world lacks an understanding of the Cross and of a divine judgment of the world. Both the human and the subhuman world are involved in sin. But the reign of evil over the hearts and institutions of men has not led to a radical and general perversion of human nature, still less to the destruction of God's good creation. The natural world has lost its vital and essential relation to the supernatural realities. Its life has been wounded and impaired and thrown into disorder. Evil is, in the deepest sense of the word, disorder—a departure from the eternal plan of the Creator operative in the nature of things. It is not primarily rebellion against God, conceived as a personal Being acting towards men in a personal way.

It is in full accord with this whole outlook that the natural world and its various spheres and activities should be regarded as possessing a relative autonomy. For while the world in its actual existence and historical forms of expression has departed from the plan of Providence, yet its essential nature remains indestructible. The common man in his various callings can himself, at least in a certain measure, know and decide for himself what is good and bad—what accords, or does not accord, with the divine ordering of life. There is thus a relative autonomy belonging to such spheres as those of marriage, economics or philosophy—an autonomy which cannot without penalty be denied or disregarded, and which even the Creator cannot alter since He has once for all established it and given it validity till the end of time. This independence is not, however, absolute. It would be a misrepresentation of the Thomist conception to treat its doctrine of the natural world in isolation. Nature and supernature complete one another and are in a continuous state of tension. The Church builds on what is given in the natural world. In the classical formulation of Thomas Aquinas, grace does not destroy nature but presupposes and perfects it. In this assertion there is implied the claim which the Roman Catholic Church cannot avoid making, to an authority over the whole of human society—not only over the souls and hearts of men, but also in social and political affairs. The Church has a direct responsibility given to it by God for the ordering of all human affairs, so far as questions of faith and morals are involved.

Though every man possesses a certain insight into the true order of things, he lacks the moral power to accomplish what he knows to be right, and his efforts need consequently to be reinforced by grace. As the sole depository of supernatural truths and the sole dispenser of sacramental grace the Church is indispensable to the welfare of society. An exclusive claim over the world is inherent in the view we are considering.

The conception of nature and supernature is not merely a theological doctrine. It is a source of spiritual strength and nourishment to devout Roman Catholics. One may cite in illustration the frequency with which Baron von Hügel recurs to it in his writings. He is never tired of describing "its quite unexhausted truth and applicability," and is convinced that a revival of religion in the modern world "depends upon a renewed grasp of this immensely resourceful outlook."[1] The recognition that God is the author of, and variously reflected in, both nature and supernature creates a polarity, a tension, in human life. It preserves the balance of religion. God is revealed *both* in the beauties of external nature and the honesties and decencies of average domestic and political life, and also in the supernatural heroism of the forgiveness of enemies and the eager acceptance of suffering. This recognition is a continual aid to prayer. It provides both a tension and a relaxation. For God is envisaged both as the God of nature, the source of all that is wholesome and homely, and as the God of supernature, the source of all that is ardent and heroic.[2]

The Roman Catholic view of the relation of the Church and the world as developed in the Thomist system is an extraordinarily powerful and impressive attempt to hold

[1] *Essays and Addresses on the Philosophy of Religion* (First Series), pp. xi, 150.
[2] Ibid. (Second Series), pp. 218–19.

in combination the other-worldly and the this-worldly ends of human life. In the words of Troeltsch, quoted by von Hügel,[1] it is just in this combination that there is to be found "the richness, the breadth and the freedom, but also the painful interior tensions and the difficult problems, of this civilization. . . . Christianity has filled the this-world ends with a far mightier and deeper life than they ever possessed before, and has nevertheless made any return to the old pagan self-limitation of the soul to these ends and to nature an impossibility or an affectation for us." The spheres of economics, politics, technology, science, and art are recognized as each possessing its own logic and going its own way, while the religious end gives to them an ultimate unity of meaning and redeems them from shallowness and futility. It does this by insisting on the soul's dedication to a holy, living God, "who, whilst containing within himself the source and meaning of all spiritual-personal life, proposes to this life, as its highest task, the full elaboration and elevation of its personality to a communion with His will." And this combination of the service of the other-worldly end and of this-worldly ends is in practice realized through a variety of callings according to men's dispositions and gifts. Some are called to devote themselves predominantly to the furtherance of human ends in the service of the State, of industry, of science, and of art. Others are called to dedicate themselves primarily to the religious end in the priesthood, in missionary service, in the performance of works of mercy, or in the contemplative life.

The differences between the Thomist doctrine of the relation of the Church and the world and the various attitudes adopted in Protestantism will engage our attention in later sections. But we may note here the

[1] *Essays and Addresses on the Philosophy of Religion* (First Series), pp. 166–7.

inseparable connection between natural law as understood in the Thomist system and an authoritative Church.
While the natural man can recognize the claims of the
moral law he must remain, owing to his sin and ignorance,
uncertain in regard to its content. The natural moral law
requires the interpretation of an authoritative Church.
Without this its contents either remain sub-Christian or
we are left with some form of religious individualism.
Moreover, man cannot by his unaided powers carry out
the teachings of the natural law, and needs the restraining
influence of a powerful Church and the support of the
means of grace which it administers. It is the Church
which must re-establish and maintain the natural order
in the world. The Thomist doctrine of natural law seems
to lead in the end inevitably to clericalism.

3. THE DEIFICATION OF THE WORLD

A view that is characteristic of the Eastern Orthodox
Churches,[1] though it has adherents in other Churches,
finds a key to the understanding of the relation of the
Church to the world in the doctrine of the Theosis or
deification of the world. In its emphasis on the transfiguration of the world and on the cosmic range of
redemption it has affinities with the Thomist conception.
This similarity is, however, mainly an outward one, since
Orthodoxy is sharply opposed to the legalistic, moralistic,
and rational elements in Roman Catholic doctrine. Its
tendency is towards a mystical identity of Church and
world rather than to a hierarchical view of lower and
higher orders in the framework of a continuity of being.

The dogma of the Incarnation is in this view the
central truth. Not justification but transfiguration is the
essential meaning of Christianity.

The great apostle in the nineteenth century of the

[1] Cf. pages 32 ff.

conception of divine humanity was the Russian philosopher Soloviev. According to his teaching man is predestined to be the universal Messiah whose task it is to redeem the world from chaos by uniting it with God. Man is the priest of God in so far as he sacrifices his own will, his human selfishness. He is king of the subhuman world, subjecting it to the divine law. And he is the prophet of ultimate unity when he aims at "the absolute unity of existence and progressively realizes it by the joint work of grace and free will, thereby gradually transforming nature separated from God into the universal and complete integration in Him which it originally possessed."[1] Jesus Christ is the spiritual and absolute man. In Him God was fully incarnate, and a new stage began in the process of the transfiguration and deification of the world through the union of God and man.

The Church, in the view of Orthodoxy, is not an institution, but a new life in Christ and with Christ, "a unity of life with all creation, communion with all human beings."[2] Its task in relation to the world is to penetrate it from within. The world is transformed by the sacramental activities of the Church. It is not the task of the Church to interfere with social life or with politics, but the more it draws its members into its sacramental communion the more will its influence be felt in the world. The Church is the soul of the world, and the more it grows the more is it able to assimilate elements of the world to itself. This is what is meant by the everlasting act of the Incarnation. "By means of this interior action, a whole world of Christian 'values' is spread abroad in the State, in economics, in civilization; thus is formed what is called the *Spirit* of an epoch."[3]

---

[1] *La Russie et l'Eglise Universelle*, quoted in Pfleger, *Wrestlers with Christ*, pp. 241-2.
[2] Bulgakov, *The Orthodox Church*, p. 106.　　　　[3] Ibid., p. 170.

4. OPPOSITION BETWEEN THE CHURCH AND THE WORLD

The Thomist view, as we have seen, holds firmly to the unity of God as Redeemer and Creator, to the consistency of the divine will manifested in the whole of the created world, to the essential connection between the Church and human affairs, and to the responsibility of the Church for the world. The protest against this doctrine by the Churches of the Reformation of the sixteenth century may be summed up in the words of Anselm of Canterbury: *Nondum considerasti quanti ponderis sit peccatum.* Sin does not mean merely a defect in being, a departure from the true nature of things, a weakness of the will and a darkening of the understanding, but an enslavement of the heart of man by the dark powers of evil, a severance of the personal relationship with God and with one's neighbour, and as a result of this an irremediable disruption and conflict in human life as a whole. The whole world lies in the evil one. This assertion has a radical and total meaning. Not only wrongs deliberately committed and social chaos, but also the noblest morality and the highest religious aspirations bear witness to man's lost condition. Everything is subject to the corrupting influence of the self-seeking will which refuses to surrender itself unreservedly to the love of the Creator. There is no way of salvation which leads from man to God; no ascending scale of moral effort and religious practice by which man can restore the lost personal fellowship with God. The incarnation of the Son of God led to the Cross, and it is in this fact that the fundamental character of the world is disclosed. The world is contrary to God and to His anointed. The Church, as the bearer of the gospel of God's forgiveness, and as the home of the new fellowship of love which God Himself creates, stands in sharp contrast over against the world.

This sense of the profound opposition between the Church and the world resulting from all that the Crucifixion implies has been in many forms of Protestantism a central and living conviction, which has determined the attitude of Christians in all their personal and social relations. The Churches on the continent of Europe, in the light of their experiences since the war, have gained a new understanding of the problem that is involved—a problem felt by Marcion with such intensity that he was driven to regard God the Redeemer and God the Creator as irreconcilable opponents.

It is in the tragic drama of sin and redemption that the ultimate meaning of human life is disclosed. Justification by faith alone is in this view the heart and substance of the Christian gospel. Salvation is the initiative of the free, sovereign love of God. The emancipation of man from subjection to the dark, destructive powers of evil and his deliverance from the prison-house of his egocentricity into a life of sonship and personal fellowship with God—these are the supreme realities which constitute the substance and power of the gospel. The Church is the place where this active, self-giving, sovereign love of God is proclaimed, a community of sinful men in which this love is the ruling power. An immense tension is thus introduced into the relation between this radically new fellowship of love and the life of the world. There has resulted a tendency prominent in, but not confined to, Lutheranism to regard the Church and the world as two separate and distinct spheres.

The traditional Lutheran understanding of the problem of the Church and the world is bound up with the question of the relation between the law and the gospel. It has already been pointed out that the understanding of the gospel as the restoration of the severed personal relation between God and man is incompatible with the doctrine of nature and supernature. This applies especially to the understanding of the law as an immanent divine law implanted in man's constitution, through which by moral effort aided by sacramental grace he can step by step arrive at the final goal of mystical union with God. This belief was regarded by the Reformers as a deception of Satan. The law and the works to which it prompts only confirm man in his self-righteousness and in his belief in his natural goodness or moral perfectibility, or alternatively drive him to despair. The psychological situation of the world is consequently one of oscillation between pride and despair. What Christ accomplishes in his Church is the redemption of man from the law and its works. The existence of the Church in the world is not, therefore, the confirmation of an existing moral law, the fulfilment of which becomes possible through the infusion of new energy, but a new and marvellous manifestation of spontaneous love.

One form in which this view of the sharp opposition between the Church and the world has found expression —not only among Lutherans but in other Churches also— is in an individualistic type of Christianity, which regards the gospel as having to do only with the salvation of individual souls and looks on participation in the affairs of the world as irrelevant or questionable. The Church is thought of as an ark in which saved souls may find refuge from a world that is doomed to destruction. The influence of the Church on the community is restricted to the manifestation of love in private relations with individuals and in ministering to the needs of the sick and the poor.

The prevailing tendency in Lutheranism has been, as we have already seen,[1] to regard the spheres of the temporal order as having their own standards and norms. The task of the Church is to inculcate in its members the

---

[1] Pages 72 ff.

duty of fulfilling their responsibilities in the world and of obeying the divinely appointed authorities. The Church has no right to interfere in worldly matters or to establish laws for the world. The world will remain world till the coming of Christ.

In the recent writings of Professor Gogarten, Professor Hirsch, and others, the traditional Lutheran doctrine has been given a fresh interpretation in what looks like a new version of the doctrine of natural law. Stress is laid on the independence of the world as against the Church. This is not to be understood as meaning that the world is independent of God. On the contrary, there is found in the world a revelation of the will of the Creator. This is manifested in the events of history and in the immanent laws which determine the working of the various forms of human association. A sharp distinction is made between God as Redeemer and God as Creator. Christian love is not directly applicable to the life of society. Social and political life is a sphere outside the competence of the Church. Life in the fellowship of the Church is a source of new power and energy. The Church is a source of fresh inspiration, but creates no new aims or norms for personal and social action different from those of the national ethos. The order of society and the determination of its purposes is the task of the political authority and of human reason. In unquestioning trust in the hidden working of Providence in the course of history, the Christian in public affairs acts in accordance with the same norms as non-Christians, and cannot do otherwise, since the connection between the will of the Creator and the will of the Redeemer is hidden and will be revealed only in the world to come. With varying degrees of consistency the upholders of this view deny to the gospel any universal claim or specific content. The strength of their position is a strong sense of the stubbornness and inertia of social evil. This view stands at the opposite pole from a superficial optimism which attempts by moral effort to transform the world into the Kingdom of God.

It is more particularly in the *Volk*, or nation, that these thinkers find the decisive expression of the divine will for conduct in this earthly life. In loyal obedience to the earthly authorities constituted by God a man can best live and serve his neighbour. The nations are the instruments of God's purpose in history and the concrete embodiments of His will. Unconditional fellowship with God imposes on the Christian the unconditional obligation to be utterly faithful to the earthly life with all the obligations which it involves. This view makes it possible to regard the national political order as hallowed by God, and yet at the same time to regard it equally clearly as a mundane and transitory matter. The grave danger, by no means confined to any one country, of such an attitude is that the Church should sink to the level of being nothing more than an instrument of national policy.

It must be made clear, however, that there are other Lutherans who totally repudiate these doctrines and regard them as highly dangerous. Dr. Werner Wiesner, in a paper contributed to the forthcoming volume on *Christian Faith and the Common Life*, rejects decisively the whole doctrine of the orders as being in their historical givenness a manifestation of the will of God. The Bible knows no such doctrine. Its reference is always to the will and law of God. All institutions are human institutions, and derive their authority neither from themselves nor from being part of a divine plan. Law possesses authority only in so far as it is the expression of *God's* law. The norm for the spheres of the common life is found, not in natural law, but only in the Biblical revelation. This norm it is the task of the Church to proclaim. Whether or not its message falls on deaf ears is not its concern. That must be left in the hands of God.

5. RELAXATION OF THE TENSION

Those into whose minds has broken the mystery and miracle of the Cross as the supreme reality of human existence cannot henceforward view the world otherwise than in its light. It becomes the great and impassable dividing line between the natural and the spiritual. The goods of this world can have only a relative and transient value.

Yet over against this overwhelming, redeeming act of God, with its transvaluation of all values, there must be set the work of God as Creator—the dear earth, the colours and shapes of things, the glimpses of entrancing beauty, the wonders and fascination of nature and of the habits of living things, the unceasing and absorbing activity of man. Has God, who created man to replenish and subdue the earth, who gave him craftsmanship and skill and made him "cunning to work in gold, and in silver, and in brass, and in iron,"[1] who implanted in him the genius of discovery and the capacity for high adventure, ceased to take pleasure in the work of His hands? Is He unmindful of the daily tasks and fidelities of those

> That with weak virtues, weaker hands,
> Sow gladness on the peopled lands,
> And still with laughter, song and shout
> Spin the great wheel of earth about?[2]

Hence, over against what is felt to be a too exclusive concentration on the central and commanding realities of sin and redemption, we find in Christian history the endeavour to reach an interpretation of the relation of the Church and the world, which gives a religious

[1] 2 Chron. ii. 7.   [2] R. L. Stevenson, *Our Lady of the Snows.*

significance to the manifold interests and activities of the world, and provides a place within the Christian outlook for a Christian humanism that is sensitive to all the movement and colour of the drama of human existence. "Religion can only be fresh and vital," it is maintained, "a spring of spontaneous inspiration such as can redeem, direct and fertilize the manifold life and interests of the world, if it is in vivid and sympathetic response to the fascinating values and opportunities, the rich and ever-widening claims and tasks of our absorbing and many-coloured society."[1]

The task of interpreting the whole of life in the light of the revelation in Christ is especially necessary in our time since, in spite of disillusionments and tendencies to pessimism, the modern mind is possessed by a sense of the vast sweep and range of the cosmic progress and by the immense opportunities which lie open to human endeavour. With unabated and restless energy the human race continues to address itself to the mastery of the forces of nature and the control and direction of the course of human life. A religion which has little or nothing to say about the manifold interests and activities which absorb men's waking hours can have no meaning for the actual life which they have to live. The Church cannot abandon the attempt to provide an ethic of civilization without relapsing into a position of irrelevance and insignificance in relation to the life of the world which is incompatible with its faith in God's sovereignty and fatherly care. The endeavour must be renewed in every age.

It seems impossible to many Christian minds to think of God's activity in the world exclusively in terms of the redemption wrought in Christ. We must be on our guard, wrote a distinguished leader of the Church in commenting on an earlier draft of this paper, against "putting too

---

[1] F. R. Barry, *Relevance of Christianity*, p. 135.

much on Christianity." The whole course of history, he would hold, is inspired, and mankind is being led into a possession of the truth by other agents than the Church. This view has affinities with the Lutheran doctrine of the two spheres, with the difference of accent that there is a disposition in this case to regard the activity of God in the temporal sphere as co-ordinate and congruous with His redeeming activity in Christ, while the Lutheran tendency is to regard the course of events in the natural world as having no connection with the Gospel of love, and as the operation of a hidden God, whose purpose will be fully revealed only in the world to come.

The religious truth which the upholders of the view we are considering desire to conserve and assert is "the vital significance of the material and temporal world to the eternal spirit." The universe is sacramental, as the Archbishop of York, from whom these words are quoted, contends, in the sense that the values found in the historical sphere are such as belong essentially to the eternal. When we think of the world, "with its aspirations and heroisms, its beauty and its love, we must needs say that these have value for God as the only alternative to saying that God is inadequate, or inferior, to the world which has proceeded from His creative act." It is only in this sacramental view of the universe "that there is given hope of making human both politics and economics, and of making effectual both faith and love."[1]

Experience has shown the tendency of religion, in proportion as it is intense, to become narrow and bigoted and to manifest harsh and unlovely features. The corrective which restores to life its true balance, breadth, and sanity comes from occupation with the activities of natural existence and from the discipline of concrete tasks. If religious belief is to be kept free from onesidedness and

[1] *Nature, Man and God*, pp. 493, 480, 486.

perversion, it is in constant need of criticism from without. If God is not absent from the world which He has created, if He is at work in the lives and undertakings even of those who do not call upon His name, the profound distinction between the Church and the world cannot be treated as identical with the difference between two sociological groups. What is said of the Church in its true nature does not necessarily apply to the Church as institution. The secular world is not only the sphere in which God's will has to be fulfilled, but has a religious significance of its own as the corrective of all ecclesiastical or priestly pretensions. It is a standing protest against the claim of any Church to be, as an institution, the sole channel of God's grace. Belief in the God and Father of our Lord Jesus Christ is hard to reconcile with the idea that He has left the world entirely to itself and is interested only in the fortunes of ecclesiastical Christianity.

It is easy to see how any relaxation of the tension between the world of redemption and the natural world is in danger of leading to an emasculation of the gospel and to the secularization of the Church, and history is evidence how often and how widely this has taken place. When this happens, and the Church becomes conformed to the world and its ways, the substance and saving power of the gospel have evaporated. None would be more ready than many of the strongest advocates of the view under consideration to recognize that the Cross cannot be taken out of Christianity without changing it beyond recognition. The Christian salvation means redemption from the world, with its standards and values. The demand of Christ is always absolute. Without the note of *contemptus mundi* there is no authentic Christianity.

Asceticism is at all times and in all circumstances an essential ingredient in every Christian life that is worthy of the name. Where this note is absent the profession of

Christianity degenerates into a spineless amiability and ineffectual goodness. There have been periods in the history of the Church when the evils of the world were so gross that they could be combated only by a stern austerity. "The resolute renunciation of the world," as Harnack reminds us, "was really the first thing which made the Church competent and strong to tell upon the world. Then, if ever, was the saying true: 'He who would do anything for the world must have nothing to do with it.' Revolutions are not effected with rose-water, and it was a veritable revolution to overthrow polytheism and to establish the majesty of God and goodness in the world."[1]

6. THE RULE OF GOD

We have already considered one broad tendency of thought about the relation of the Church to the world, deriving its inspiration from the ideas of the Reformation. This has found expression in a variety of forms, and more particularly in Lutheranism, though the attitude is not that of all Lutherans, and is also that of many Christians belonging to other Churches besides the Lutheran. We must now turn our attention to another main type of thought resulting from the Reformation. This has found expression chiefly in Calvinism, though in its broad features it also has adherents among Lutherans and the members of other Churches not deeply influenced by the Calvinist tradition.

This view, no less than the other, is rooted in the conviction that salvation is from the first to last a personal act of the self-communication of God to a sinful and lost world. But, unlike the other view, it does not interpret the claim of Christ to universal dominion over the whole

[1] *The Mission and Expansion of Christianity*, I, p. 98.

world in an exclusively eschatological sense and place its realization in the future, but rather as imposing on the Church a missionary task directed towards influencing the whole life of society. As the ambassador and servant of its living, risen Lord the Church is the instrument of His rule, and is called to bear its witness throughout the whole world and in all spheres of life, including those of business and politics.

The relation of the Church to the world is thus one of dramatic tension, where the boundaries are continually shifting, where the fortunes of the struggle vary, and where new fronts are constantly being formed. There can thus be no question of the Church withdrawing itself from the world or regarding the conditions and happenings of society as irrelevant to its own life. The love of Christ constrains the Church to enter as deeply and as widely as possible into the life of mankind. The new fellowship with God has a spontaneous urge to express itself in new social relations and in new ways of dealing with material things.

This activism in relation to the world has its source and its criterion in a humble and joyous receptivity. The Church encounters the world not primarily with a demand or an ideal, but with the proclamation of a gift—a gift so rich and comprehensive that it has a relevance for the whole of life.

There is a strong eschatological strain in this view of the relation of the Church and the world. It is far removed from any optimistic belief in the progressive realization of the rule of God within the course of human history. It is aware, like the writers of the New Testament, that the opposition of the powers of evil will increase in strength in proportion as the Church is loyal to its divine commission in the conflict with falsehood and wrong. The Church and the world will be opposed to one another to the end of time. The final victory will not be achieved on earth. But the hope of the transcendent accomplishment of God's rule, of which the Church is only the first fruits, does not lead to a complacent acquiescence in things as they are. It is an ever-present vision which nerves endeavour and inspires to fresh adventure.

The existence of the Church implies a complete transvaluation of all the values which are current in the world. The Church has its own distinctive message and its own standards which it presents to the world. The Church cannot, therefore, give its unqualified endorsement even to the noblest endeavours for social justice and international peace without first asking how far these will further the reign of Christ. This does not diminish in any way the active responsibility of the Church for the affairs of the world. But this responsibility has its own perspective and its own categories of judgment. These are the realities of evil and of love, and not those of hedonistic happiness or of a purely negative peace. The proclamation of the Kingdom of God is the source and centre of Christian action but not a goal which can be comprehended or realized by men. The formulation of programmes of Christian action and the adoption of concrete aims are not precluded. But these are incidental and temporary in character, since they are always related to the existing situation.

It may lead to fruitful discussion and bring before us certain illuminating and instructive contrasts if we set over against the view described in the preceding paragraphs an alternative conception of the establishment of God's rule which has met with wide acceptance and has influenced the attitude and action of many Churches and of multitudes of individual Christians. We may for convenience describe this as the evolutionary, optimistic Christian view of the world. It will serve our purpose best to begin by sharpening the contrasts, and for this reason to state the alternative in its extremer forms of expression. It is important to realize that the issues we are about to consider are the occasion of the acutest differences within the oecumenical Christian movement; it is at this point that the difficulties of agreement are greatest, both in faith and action. But it must also be emphasized that on these very issues the lines continually cross, and that the upholders of one view, as here expounded, would very often not only not wish to deny elements of truth in the opposite view but would strongly affirm them as an essential part of their own faith.

The picture of the world presented by modern science, with an ever-multiplying wealth of detail, as the result of a continuous process unfolding and developing itself by an inner necessity, has in recent generations laid powerful hold of the minds and imaginations of men. It seemed natural to regard Christianity as the culmination of a universal process which was at the same time God's revelation of Himself to man and man's discovery of God. Among recent writers we find this conception determining the outlook of the Bishop of Durham in his Gifford Lectures on *Christian Morality*, which he maintains to be at once *natural*, *developing*, and *final*; and of Professor Raven in his Riddell Lectures on *Evolution and the Christian Conception of God*, where Christ is presented as the consummation and completion of "the age-long world-wide purpose of creation," and it is maintained that to regard Him thus "as typical, representative and illuminating, not as alien, intrusive or confounding," is not to honour or worship Him the less, but to find in His revelation "a new coherence, a new validity, a new majesty."[1]

Similar ideas underlay what came to be known as the Social Gospel in America. Walter Rauschenbusch, its

---

[1] Page 31.

most brilliant exponent, explicitly connects it with "the universal reign of law, the doctrine of evolution, the control of nature by man, which are among the most influential convictions of modern life."[1] Its dominant inspiration is the Kingdom of God conceived as a goal to be realized within the temporal order. The phrase which continually recurs in the literature of the movements inspired by these ideas is that of building the Kingdom of God on earth. The end is conceived as the creation of a world of social justice, peace, brotherhood, and plenty. A recent resolution of the General Council of the Congregational and Christian Churches of the United States setting up a Council for Social Action reads: "Believing that the Church will find itself as it loses itself in the struggle to achieve a warless, just and brotherly world, we launch this venture, dedicating ourselves to unremitting work for a day in which all men find peace, security and abundant life." The kingdom of heaven on earth is a world "from which fear and want are banished," in which there is "mutual respect among individuals, personal growth and social responsibility."[2] It would be possible to multiply indefinitely utterances of Christian gatherings in which these ideas find expression and evoke enthusiastic and passionate assent.

The faith which inspires the movement we are describing may, perhaps, be briefly summarized as follows. Christianity is essentially the revelation of the infinite value of human personality and of love as the supreme principle of life. Community, or the true social order, means persons living in fellowship and love. Christian loyalty requires that these principles should be applied to every relationship of life. Brotherhood means sharing

---

[1] *A Theology of the Social Gospel*, p. 23.
[2] See the literature of the Council for Social Action, 287 Fourth Avenue, New York.

in material things as well as in spiritual. The Kingdom of God is the progressive realization of the reign of love in human affairs. Every economic, social or political system has to be judged by the measure in which it hinders or facilitates the free growth of persons and of fellowship and mutual love and trust between them.

The fact that there is much in this statement to which many Christians with a wholly different theological outlook from that of some advocates of the Social Gospel would subscribe—with some differences, no doubt, of phraseology and emphasis—shows how great is the need for further clarification and mutual understanding.

The strongly monistic character of this evolutionary interpretation of Christianity, in some at least of its expressions, its optimistic view of human nature, its minimizing of the distinction between the Church and the world and its often exclusive emphasis on this-worldly ends, provoke in other quarters the most vehement dissent and strongest opposition.

We may try now to draw out certain contrasts which may help to illuminate the whole of our discussion. The two attitudes, which though they are both concerned with the establishment of the rule of God are yet so sharply opposed to one another, have their roots in different conceptions of God and of His relation to the world. In the one view God is conceived of as the Creator, "whose act of creation does not exhaust His being, who remains absolutely free, not limited or conditioned by His creation. It is His will, not a principle or law of rational or moral character, that sets the norm for man's life. He is therefore personal, for it is as dynamic and sovereign will, truly distinct from one's own will, that man comes to know Him."[1] God is in His nature

[1] W. A. Visser 't Hooft, *The Background of the Social Gospel in America*, pp. 169–70.

mysterious, unfathomable, and incomprehensible to human understanding. His ways are hidden. He has indeed revealed Himself in Christ, and man has this clear light by which to guide his steps. But God's purpose always reaches beyond what man with his limited insight and understanding believes to be good and right. This emphasis on the sovereignty and transcendence of God is an essential element in Christianity, and at the same time the spring of social progress. For a religion that is fully at home in society, and is merely the expression of the prevailing values and aspirations, has nothing important to say to it. Only from that which lies beyond all culture and conventional morality can there come an effective and transforming criticism of the self and of society. Human effort and aspiration must be brought to the bar of God's searching judgment to find in submission to it purification, renewal, and fresh outreach.

In the other view the distance between God and man is lessened. Love and goodness as manifested in human life are the essential qualities of God. There is a norm common to God and man. God is the indwelling law of the universe manifest in human reason and goodness. God's plan for the world tends to be identified with human purposes. "The old gulf which separated man from God is bridged, and instead of the dramatic conception that mankind is in revolution against its Creator there comes the optimistic idea that there is a happy comradeship in the common undertaking of building a fairer and brighter world."[1]

This attitude is plainly liable, and has often succumbed, to the danger of reducing the Christian gospel, with its inexhaustible and mysterious depths and overwhelming paradoxes, to a programme of humanitarian reform and

[1] W. A. Visser 't Hooft, *The Background of the Social Gospel in America*, p. 175.

shallow meliorism. Yet in its more serious forms it is contending for a truth which many would hold to be as essential to Christianity as insistence on the divine transcendence. Man's normal perceptions of value must be in some measure true. If God was not revealed in the affections and loyalties of human intercourse, men would be incapable of understanding His revelation in Christ. The divine method in dealing with men is that of persuasion. The only ultimate authority is that which makes its appeal to insight. What claims obedience is that which is recognized to possess intrinsic truth and worth.

Between these two poles the Christian life must continually revolve. We have no way of understanding and expressing the love of God except through such acts as our finite and sinful nature is capable of performing. And yet to equate the divine love which passes understanding with what we understand by love and with our small and shallow programmes is to withdraw ourselves from the judgment that has power to shatter our complacency and remake us as new creatures in Christ. The aims and activities of the limited communities of nature and history are, as Professor Reinhold Niebuhr has said, "both the promise of, and a peril to, the love of the Kingdom of God."[1]

A second contrast is between the emphasis laid in the two views on the action of God and on the action of men in the establishment of God's rule. On the one hand is the desire to assert that the Kingdom of God is not a human enterprise to be brought about by human effort and that God alone can establish it. It is God's gift and creation, and He will bring it to pass at His own time and in His own way. On the other side the emphasis is laid on the fact that God uses men for the accomplishment of His

[1] In a paper contributed to the forthcoming volume on *Christian Faith and the Common Life*.

purposes and seeks their co-operation. Here again justice must be done to each of these two truths. A sense of human insufficiency is inseparable from any genuine Christian experience. Life is transformed when a man awakens to the fact that in the work he has to do he is not dependent on his own powers but on forces of truth and goodness outside himself in which he can participate. It is this fact of participation in a life and purpose that are not his own that alone eliminates the element of presumption which must otherwise taint and vitiate every effort to save or reform the world. On the other hand, it is no less necessary to hold firmly to the truth that it has pleased God to choose men to be the instruments of carrying out His purpose of redemption for the world and that He waits for their response in faith and obedience.

Thirdly, we are again confronted with the fundamental issue of the difference between the law and the gospel. What modern Protestantism has done, it is contended on the one side, is to transform the gospel into a legal code, to substitute ideals for the proclamation of redeeming facts and of the advent of a new reality, and to see no more in Christ than the teacher of a higher morality. The danger of turning Christianity into a new law is always present, and throughout the history of the Church Christians have constantly yielded to the temptation. To do this is to pervert its nature and to destroy its power. Yet those, on the other hand, who insist on the primacy of the gospel are in danger sometimes of forgetting that the gospel as the revelation of a new world has inescapable ethical implications that confront both the individual and society with the necessity of decision. The God who has revealed His grace and forgiveness in Christ is also a righteous and holy God who makes a claim on the whole man, transforming his motives, his interests, and his ideals. It must be recognized also that many whose utterances might lay them open to the criticism that they have forgotten that Christianity is primarily a gospel have been inspired by a Christlike passion for righteousness and have earned the commendation of those who are doers of the Word and not hearers only.

A final contrast relates to the agents by whom Christian social action is to be carried out. The one view, which draws no sharp distinction between the Church and the world, looks to the common action of all men of goodwill. Its programmes tend to be such as may be expected to win the support of Christians and non-Christians alike. Both knowledge of the right ends and power to realize them may be counted on in the general community. In the other view, it is the Church that has been chosen by God as the vehicle of His revelation and the instrument for the realization of His purposes. It is the true centre of social renewal, and it can become this in fact in so far as it places itself unreservedly at God's disposal. There can be no Christian social order where there are not first Christian men. The social implications of the Christian message offer guidance to the Church in regard to the ordering of its own life and its relation to the world, but offer no cure for the problems of the world, acute and pressing as they are, apart from Christ.

CHAPTER VII

THE FUNCTIONS OF THE CHURCH

THE responsibilities of the Church in relation to the general life of the community and the social, political, and international order cannot be detached from their roots in the *being* of the Church and the total expression of its life. The Church ministers to the needs of society not so much by the exercise of this or that particular function as by its whole existence. While it is necessary for practical purposes to distinguish different functions of the Church, all its functions are related to one another and each requires for its effective exercise the fulfilment of the others. If one is permitted to languish, the efficacy of the others is impaired. There is no panacea for the evils from which the world is suffering. The influence of the Church on society is the result of the faithfulness of a multitude of individuals, each fulfilling loyally the task which at any given moment he is called to perform.

The functions of the Church are determined not by the needs of any particular historical situation, but by its divine commission. It is also true, however, that each fresh experience through which men pass may contribute to a new understanding of God's purpose for the Church. If God is the living God we must expect that through an honest facing of the demands of the contemporary situation new light will be vouchsafed. It is an encouragement to hope for this that we are permitted to seek for light in an oecumenical fellowship in which each of the Churches may contribute to the common deliberations the gift of its own distinctive tradition and experience.

1. THE CONSTITUTIVE FUNCTIONS OF THE CHURCH

It is the common faith of Christians that the Church owes its existence to an act of God in history. It derives its being from God. It draws its nourishment and sustenance from God. Its primary functions, therefore, are those which relate to the divine source of its life—the acts by which it is ever anew constituted as a Church and takes fresh possession, so to speak, of the Reality which makes it what it is. These functions have a receptive and an active side.

(a) Receptive

We were reminded in an earlier chapter, in words quoted from Baron von Hügel, that religion begins and ends with the *given*. The fundamental attitude of the Christian is consequently that of receiving. This truth is insisted on with equal decisiveness in both the Catholic and the Reformation conceptions of the worship of the Church. It is asserted in the Protestant doctrine that the Word and the Sacraments constitute the Church. The Church is a place, or rather the one place, where self-confident, autonomous man is reminded that with all his proud autonomy he is not his own, but he stands in the presence and power of Another, with whom he has to come to terms.[1] In the Catholic conception of worship there is a similar insistence on the priority and prevenience of God. The central place is filled by the Eucharist. The sacrifice of the Mass is something objectively given independently of any mood or state of feeling or desert on the part of the worshipper.

The acts of reception by which the Church ever anew constitutes itself a Church are the hearing of the Word and the receiving of the sacraments. To listen to the

[1] Thurneysen, *Das Wort Gottes und die Kirche*, pp. 64, 102.

Word is to open the mind and heart to the message of the grace and truth that came by Jesus Christ. This truth enshrined in the Bible is made living and effectual by the Holy Spirit. Only by the continuous exposure of the whole being to its transfiguring influence can we fulfil the apostolic injunction not to be conformed to this world, but to be transformed by the renewing of our minds. It is not merely individual members of the Church, but the Church as a whole in the person of its teachers and leaders and rulers that has thus to listen to God's Word that it may be progressively converted to the mind of Christ.

We misunderstand the significance of Christian worship if we think primarily of its subjective aspects. The central thing is not the elevation of the soul to God in pious thoughts, but the new orientation of life which follows from the acknowledgment of the reality of God, and from the deliverance through His redeeming grace from self-centredness, which is the essential, fundamental sin and evil and the corruption of all morality.

(b) Active

Corresponding to the receptive acts by which the Church is ever constituted afresh, there are the active functions in which, through its appointed officers, the Church mediates what it has received. These are, first, the proclamation of the Gospel—not merely in preaching and addresses, but in acts of worship and deeds of mercy and love that declare its central message—and, secondly, in the administration of the sacraments, with their unfailing witness to the objectivity and reality of God's redemption.

It is the constitutive functions of the Church that it is intended to safeguard when the Church is defined in the Thirty-nine Articles of the Church of England and in the Confessio Augustana, as the congregation of faithful men in which the pure Word of God is preached (or the Gospel is rightly taught) and the Sacraments duly administered. Without the exercise of these essential functions in which the Church renews its life, the Church would no longer be a Church in the Christian sense. But this is not to say that the preaching of the Gospel and the Sacraments are the only expression of the life of the Church. They are the source of a new life which is meant to manifest itself in new attitudes and behaviour and to bring about transformations in the life of society. The deepest truths are often the most dangerous. Insistence on the essential, constitutive functions may lead too easily in practice, as we have already seen,[1] to a disastrous ecclesiasticizing of the Church, so that it becomes primarily an affair and interest of the clergy and pastors and theologians rather than a community of redeemed men and women joyfully serving God in the ordinary concerns of the common life.

2. FUNCTIONS RELATING TO THE EXPRESSION AND REALIZATION OF THE LIFE OF THE CHURCH

(a) The Church as a Community of Worship

The essential meaning of the Christian gospel is redemption. Life has been given a new centre. The centre of the Christian's life is no longer himself but God. The deepest expression of the new life is consequently worship and adoration. We are concerned here with man's response to God's act and gift, which in its objective reality we have already considered. Worship is the response of believing men in adoration and joyous self-dedication to God's revelation of Himself and to His redeeming grace. The Church is by its nature a worshipping community, and it is a necessary function of the Church as an organized society to provide opportunities for common and public

[1] Pages 113 ff.

worship and to educate its individual members in the spirit and practice of worship.

Worship is not only the natural expression and language of the Christian soul, but the fountain and source of creative activities. Without continual reference to an ultimate standard and absolute judgment all work tends to lose its significance. The self becomes identified with the objects of its pursuit. Our souls shrink to the dimensions of the things that we do. The witness of the Church draws reality and depth from its worship.

These rich possibilities of worship can be realized only in so far as faith lays hold of the reality of God. The danger is always present that the worshipper may become occupied with his own states and feelings, and be content to have his emotions quickened and elevated in private prayer or in congregational worship while his will and behaviour remain wholly uninfluenced. It is at this point that the modern attack on the life of religion as an evasion of reality contains a sting of truth. We ought to be under no illusions in regard to the extent to which worship may be, and too often is, an escape from the burdens and vexations of life into a world of soothing hopes and transient and ineffective aspirations.

Christian worship when true to its own nature rises above these dangers. It does not consist in the aesthetic contemplation of the universe nor in a flight into an imaginary world in which compensation may be found for the too heavy burdens and trials of this earthly life. It is not "a contemplative immersion in Being, or a quietistic denegation of the will, but an active dedication of the will to a God who is overflowingly alive, and has positive ends for the world and opens up an immense movement for this same world."[1] Those who have experienced, even on rare occasions, the realities of prayer,

[1] Troeltsch, *Gesammelte Schriften*, Vol. II, p. 636.

know that such moments have been the most creative and
fruitful in their lives. Worship is adoration issuing in
action, and the unity of adoration and action transforms
life into a sacrament. A worshipping community dedicated
to the fulfilment of God's purpose becomes the means
through which God's purpose may be realized in the world
in all the relationships of human life.

The offering, both individual and corporate, of the
self to God in service and sacrifice has always been a
central element in Christian worship, and fills a large
place in Christian liturgies. "The response of the human
creature to the Divine is summed up in sacrifice; the
action which expresses more fully than any other his
deep, if uncomprehended, relation to God. . . . Without
it worship may easily degenerate into emotional admira-
tion; and, on the other hand, the 'spiritual' sacrifice
without concrete embodiment lacks at least one element
of costliness, and is out of touch with the here and now
realities of human life."[1]

It is essential to true worship that it should not become
detached from the practical responsibilities of life, of
which it is meant to be the consecration and inspiration.
Corporate worship would seem to require, in order to be
fully real, a sharing by the worshippers of experience and
need with one another, and also an explicit reference to
particular tasks and difficulties, for meeting which the
common worship supplies inspiration and strength. To
worship truly with other men we must know them as men,
whose burdens we may share. The requirements of true
corporate worship are not fully met by large congregational services. These need to be revitalized and enriched
by the worship of smaller groups in which a more intimate
human fellowship is possible.

In so far as it achieves its true and full purpose, the

[1] Evelyn Underhill, *Worship*, pp. 47–8.

worship of the Church may be regarded as the most potent and fruitful form of social action. Who can tell what life-giving energies may through it be released, or what hidden secret forces may be set in motion spreading from person to person and insensibly transforming the thought and spirit of the age? But this can take place, it would seem, only if the connection with actual life is never allowed to be lost; if worship imparts a significance to the daily round; if it consecrates and illuminates with meaning the relations of family and neighbourhood, recreation and friendship, and the various interests of the common life; if those who kneel at the altar are in that act re-dedicated to the service of God and man and go forth with loins regirt and sword unsheathed to fight in the name of the Lord against all iniquity. To believe that such results as have been suggested can flow from worship, and that they have in fact manifested themselves in the course of Christian history must not lead us to assume that the worship of the Church to-day is active as a mighty leaven in the life of the world. To speak as we have done of the worship of the Church is a call to searching self-examination.

(b) The Church as a Community of Love

Familiarity has dulled our minds to the startling and revolutionary quality of such words as these: "He that abideth in love abideth in God, and God abideth in him." "Every one that loveth is begotten of God, and knoweth God." "Now abideth faith, hope, love, these three: and the greatest of these is love."

The Church has rightly laid stress on faith, since it is only by our personal response to God's personal call that we can be redeemed to a new life. But it has in a far less degree emphasized the other truth that the new life into

which we are called and admitted is a life of community
and love. The impression which the Church has too often
conveyed to the world is that to be a Christian means
primarily to hold certain doctrinal beliefs. Only through
the lives of some of its saints and of a relatively small
proportion of its humbler and unknown members has it
given occasion to the outside world to suppose that to be a
Christian is to be redeemed into a new sphere of being
in which love and freedom reign.

The Church is the realization of true community. Its
essential nature is fellowship between persons. It can be
the manifestation of the true meaning of community
because its life is rooted in the love of God. It is only the
love of God which can deliver us from our self-centred
isolation and set us free to love our fellow-men. The more
we struggle to overcome our egocentricity the more ego-
centric we become. Only a love that comes to us from
without and gives our lives a new centre in the One who
loves us can break the fetters of our self-love. The Church
is thus the sphere of free relations of mutual love and trust
between persons, and is meant to be the witness to the
world of the true relations of men with one another.

Christian love is something quite other than sentimental
charity or humanitarian good will or natural human comradeship. It has its spring in the costly self-giving of Christ.
It finds its objects not only in those who are attractive and
congenial, but in those who are unlovely and naturally
repellent. It loves men because it knows them to be the
objects of God's love. It sees in the other man not merely
what he is now but what he might become through the
redeeming and creative power of love.

Christian love is open-eyed to the concrete physical,
intellectual, and moral needs of men, and seeks to minister
to those needs, but it is never content to stop there.
Its aim in and through these ministries is to bring men to

Christ, in order that the deepest need of their nature may be met. The pastoral cure of souls must fill a large place in the life of the community of love. There are multitudes who are sick in soul as well as in body and in mind. Ministry to these needs is not the responsibility of the clergy and pastors alone, but of all members of the Christian community. A promising beginning has been made in some places in co-operation between the clergy and the medical profession and psychiatrists in dealing with cases of mental distress. There are many instances which call for professional, scientific advice if they are to be successfully treated, and many in which the physician recognizes that the only cure is the regeneration of the whole personality through the experience of the forgiveness of sins and the restoration of confidence in a life of childlike trust in God.

The Church should be the place where barriers of race, nationality, class, sex, and education are done away; where the unprivileged, the down-trodden, the outcast, and the despised find a welcome and feel themselves at home; a meeting-ground where those who are divided in questions of politics and economics can realize afresh their unity in loyalty to a common Lord, can discuss their differences in the reality of this fellowship and learn mutually to understand one another. In the modern disintegration of social life the Church ought to provide centres in which men can find protection, shelter, and security in the care and love of their fellow-men, and re-discover the meaning of community in the support and comradeship of a society, the members of which bear one another's burdens and seek the good of all. The Church ought also to be the place not only where support and encouragement are given to those who need it, but where the more robust and vigorous may find their individualism and self-will disciplined and tempered, and their purposes purified and strengthened in a common endeavour to learn and fulfil the will of Christ.

When we speak of the Church fulfilling this function, however, we have again to make distinctions. If we look for something which from the nature of things cannot come about we are doomed to disappointment and may lose courage. The Church as an organized society includes a multitude of persons in very different stages of growth in the Christian life, if indeed in many instances they have entered on the Christian life at all. Many of them, like the disciples of whom we read in the Acts of the Apostles, "have not so much as heard whether there be any Holy Ghost." It cannot be expected, therefore, that they should manifest in full measure the gifts of the Spirit, the chief of which is love. What we must look for, and work for, is the growth of smaller groups who will seek to realize among themselves the relations of mutual trust and support and responsibility which are characteristic of the Christian society. Such groups, while they may to begin with be small, must not become esoteric and exclusive. They must continually be seeking to enlarge their borders. The purpose of the leaven is to leaven the whole lump, but it is necessary first of all that there should be the leaven. It is futile to waste our breath in demanding that the "Church" be this or that. We have to begin with ourselves and those whom we can influence. Life becomes real when we face our own responsibilities. It has been "the few in every age who have been the soul of every reform and started every revival upon its daring course."[1] The Church has to be continually re-born as the living Church within the Church as an organized society. If within the larger body there are groups of persons actively engaged in discovering and realizing the meaning of Christian community as a fellowship of persons living

---

[1] W. F. Lofthouse, *Christianity in the Social State*, p. 144.

together in relations of mutual trust, love, obligation, and service, those outside who are brought by circumstances into touch with this life will feel its power and attraction and find Christ in and through His Church. One of the factors which has contributed most to the triumph of both Communism and National-Socialism is that they have succeeded in making fellowship and comradeship in small groups a real and living experience.

(c) The Church as a Community of Thought

It was said in an earlier chapter[2] that the Church is the abiding witness to the manifestation in history of a new reality. The grace and truth which came into the world by Jesus Christ have to find continually renewed expression both in life, as we have seen in the preceding section, and also in thought. It is the task of the Church to interpret, both to its own members and to the world outside, the meaning and implications of the Gospel which it proclaims. The interpretation in thought of a truth which is inexhaustible can never be more than fragmentary. But the striving for an understanding that is clearer, deeper, and richer can never cease.

It is one of the gravest weaknesses in the position of the Church to-day that it lacks an adequate theology. Notable contributions to theological thought are not wanting. But what we have in the main is a chaos of different, and often conflicting, private opinions and not a recognized theology of the Church. Our survey in the preceding chapter reveals how immense is the task which has yet to be undertaken.

The statement in one of the earlier drafts of this paper that perhaps the chief need of the Church to-day to equip it to fulfil its mission to society is a theology provoked much interesting comment. The laymen who commented

[2] Page 103.

on the paper, almost without exception, seized on the statement with avidity and expressed their warm agreement. One of these, who, after a distinguished public career, is devoting himself to the service of the poor, wrote in the margin that he regarded it as the most important sentence in the paper. A distinguished theologian, on the other hand, expressed his unqualified dissent. Nothing could be more perverse, he maintained, than to suppose that the hope of the world lies in theology, with its intellectualism, its abstractions, its remoteness from life, and its barren controversies. Experience shows how small is the transforming influence of even the best theology. The reformation of the Church is vastly more important than the reformation of theology. Only out of a re-born Church may we hope for the emergence of a vitalized theology.

Some further explanation is obviously needed. What the laymen want, and what the professor of theology discounts, are two different things. Speculative and critical thought divorced from life and action has certainly little or nothing to contribute to the solution of the acute problems of the modern world. But what the laymen are painfully aware of is that action is often impeded and paralysed by lack of clarity in regard to the conduct in the practical affairs of life which is demanded of a Christian. They feel the need of a more fully thought out, and more generally accepted, interpretation of the Christian understanding of life, which strives at one and the same time to conserve the purity and fullness of the Gospel and to express it in terms that are relevant to the thought, experience, and circumstances of men to-day.

In the present crisis in which the Church finds itself the response to God's call must include the response of thought. The rival systems which claim men's allegiance make their appeal to men's understanding as well as to their feelings, and must be engaged and countered in both spheres. This is necessary not only for the sake of the witness of the Church to those who are without, but in order that its own members may be established and fortified in their faith. In the fulfilment of its task the Church must call to its aid the best minds that it can command. These will include laymen as well as theologians. It is an interesting fact that the leading thinkers in the Orthodox Church in the last century were laymen.

Students of theology have an indispensable contribution to make to the task which the Church is facing. There is urgent need of a fresh orientation of theological thought and a closer and more intimate relation between theological study and the problems of to-day. It is encouraging to find the Norris-Hulse Professor of Divinity in the University of Cambridge pleading for interpreters of Christianity "who, having penetrated to the historical actuality of first-century Christianity, have received an impression of the truth in it which lies beyond the flux of time and demands to be re-stated in terms intelligible to the mind of our own age," and who will consequently seek "to grasp the whole first-century Gospel in its temporary, historical, and therefore actual, reality, and then make the bold and even perilous attempt to translate the whole into contemporary terms."[1]

Essential as is the contribution of theologians, it is no less essential for its largest fruitfulness that it should be made in living and direct contact with other types of thought and experience. One great weakness in modern life is its departmentalism. There are few things more needed than the achievement of an outlook on life which embraces and combines varied types of experience. Theological thought will acquire a new relevance to the actual life of our time, if opportunities can be created for

[1] C. H. Dodd, *The Present Task in New Testament Studies*, pp. 38, 40.

theologians to meet in personal conference with those responsible for the conduct of public affairs and of industry, with representatives of labour, with educators and members of other professions, and learn from them at what points Christian doctrine is relevant to their responsibilities, experience, problems, and needs.

The clearer understanding of the significance of Christian faith for the actual life of our time which we desiderate is not primarily a matter of scholarship and learning. It is rather the fruit of spiritual insight and understanding, and we must never allow ourselves to forget that the realities of the spiritual world may be hidden from the wise and prudent and revealed to babes. The truth we are seeking may come through prophets raised up by God to serve the needs of our generation, or it may be silently born in the minds of multitudes of plain men and women, as they loyally endeavour to do the will of Christ in the ordinary circumstances of their lives, and spread from one to another till it becomes a common possession. What we have in view is not a body of doctrinal teaching imposed from above, but a widely shared, growing clarity in regard to the true ends of life, by the light of which ordinary men and women will be able more surely to direct their steps. But the truth thus apprehended, in order to do its full work in the world, must be thought out in all its implications and defined with increasing clearness in relation to the thought and problems of the age. The task of thought is to illuminate and strengthen Christian witness and action.

We may take heart from the fact that the theology of which we have been speaking may be forged in the conflicts with the anti-Christian forces of our time. The open challenge not only to Christian belief but to Christian standards of conduct is helping to make clear what is at stake. The Christian creeds took their shape in the early centuries in the struggle with various forms of heresy. The Church was driven to declare that certain views were incompatible with the Christian understanding of life. Similarly in the struggles of to-day it may become increasingly clear to the Christian conscience that certain allegiances and certain forms of behaviour are irreconcilable with the Christian faith and with Christian loyalties. Thus by a negative path we may arrive at a clearer positive definition of what the Christian faith signifies for life to-day.

What is progressively learned must also be systematically taught. Even among professing Christians there is in many circles a profound and astonishing ignorance of what the Christian faith is. It is common to find a complete vagueness in regard to its doctrinal beliefs, its ethical demands and its social relevance. There is need for far more extended, thorough, and systematic teaching on these subjects than is at present provided.

(d) The Church as a Social Organism

Reference may be made to a further function of the Church, though we cannot enlarge upon it here. It is the function of the Church in relation to its own organization —its constitution, administration, finance, rules, and customs. This is a field in which the characteristic life of the Church ought to find significant expression. As is urged by a group which is attempting to bring about reforms in the ministry and the distribution of the revenues of the Church of England "in regard to many of the ills of contemporary society the influence of the Church can only be indirect and persuasive, but it is within our power to set our own house in order." The work of the Church is seriously impeded when its institutional life is a contradiction of the message which it proclaims. Constitutional and economic reform, when it is called for, may be "a sacrament of spiritual purpose and loyalty as no pietism can be," since "the Spirit of God always breaks into human life conspicuously at the point of action—when men and groups do without fear or delay what they know is right."[1]

3. FUNCTIONS IN RELATION TO THE WORLD

(a) Evangelization

As witness to the manifestation in history of the true meaning of human existence the Church is under an obligation to make that revelation known to all men. Though Christians have been to an extraordinary degree blind to the fact, it is impossible to hold the Christian faith of a Divine salvation for the world and at the same time to deny or question the right of all men to participate in its benefits. Christianity in the periods when it has been most alive has always been inspired by a "passion for souls."

The more we occupy ourselves with the problems of the social and political, and in particular of the international order, the plainer it becomes that one of the fundamental obstacles to a solution is the fact of complete disagreement in regard to the ultimate purposes of life. How is agreement possible in practical affairs among those who hold irreconcilable philosophies of life? The conditions prevailing in the social and political spheres are determined, in part at least, by the attitudes and decisions of persons. If the purpose of God is to be realized in these spheres, and if the Christian understanding of life is to influence social and political action, it must come about through a change in the attitudes and actions of persons. Those movements within the Church which insist on the primary necessity

[1] *Men, Money and the Ministry: A Plea for Economic Reform in the Church of England* (Longmans, Green & Co.).

of a change of the heart and mind of individuals are striking at the root of social evil. Most emphatically the conversion of individuals is not all. For, in the first place, the individual in isolation is a pure abstraction; he is inseparable from the social context, by the ideas and institutions of which he is moulded, and in which he has to act. And, secondly, the significance of conversion lies in the ends to which men are converted and the content and quality of the new life to which they commit themselves. None the less it remains true that repentance and conversion are the starting-point of the Christian life. To be a Christian is to undergo a complete change of mind. The Christian purpose in the social and political spheres can be achieved only by those who have been converted to the Christian understanding of life. While this conversion of the heart and mind is only the beginning, it is the indispensable beginning. In proportion as the Church is in earnest about its responsibilities in the social and political spheres it must address itself with renewed energy to the task of evangelism. The social order can be improved only by persons whose lives have found a new orientation. To ignore this in thought, in policy, or in practice, is to evade the realities of life and to escape into a dreamworld of fanciful imaginations and empty hopes. The evangelization of non-Christian peoples, and of the masses in Western countries which have broken completely with the Christian tradition, must always hold a central place in the life and activities of the Church.

It is unmistakably clear that the work of evangelism is not one that can be accomplished by the clergy alone. Their numbers are too few, the responsibilities resting upon them already too varied and exacting, for them to reach effectively the masses outside the Church. Those who have to be won to the Christian faith do not for the most part attend the services of the Church. If they are to be reached, they must be reached in their homes, their places of business, and their resorts of recreation. They must be won, if they are to be won at all, by their fellow-laity. The Oxford Group Movement has furnished an illustration of the possibilities of lay evangelism. Laymen are often not qualified to undertake systematic preaching, which demands theological training. But they can bear witness to that which they have found and which has illuminated and changed their lives. To multiply such witnesses is the task to which the Church must address itself, if it would fulfil its evangelistic mission to the world.

(b) The Ministry of Mercy and Kindness

The greatest service that the Church can render to men is to bring them to Christ, in whom their deepest needs are met. But it renders this service not merely by preaching, but by acts which express and confirm the spoken message. In deeds of mercy and kindness, as well as in word, the Church proclaims to men the message of God's redeeming love.

Christ declared that the characteristic of the new society which He founded, differentiating it from all others, was that its members were servants of one another, following the example of the Son of Man who "came not to be ministered unto, but to minister and to give his life a ransom for many." In the washing of his disciples' feet he gave an example that "ye also should do as I have done unto you." The test to be applied at the final judgment is whether men have fed the hungry, given drink to the thirsty, clothed the naked, visited the sick and the prisoner. The lesson sank deep into the minds of His disciples. The epistles are full of exhortations to remember the poor, to visit the fatherless and the widows, to exercise hospitality, to show mercy and compassion.

How large a part the ministry of mercy filled in the life of the early Church one may see from the chapter on "The Gospel of Love and Charity" in Harnack's *Mission and Expansion of Christianity*.[1] The headings of the sections of this chapter are sufficient to show the range of the activities—almsgiving in general, the support of widows or orphans, the support of the sick, the infirm, and the disabled, the care of prisoners, the care of poor people needing burial, the care of slaves, the care of those visited by great calamities, the care of brethren on a journey and of churches in poverty or in peril. The story is summed up in the words, "The new language on the lips of Christians was the language of love. But it was more than a language, it was a thing of power and action. The Christians really considered themselves brothers and sisters and their actions corresponded to this belief." The Gospel was proclaimed not only in word but in deed. Tertullian could claim "It is our care for the helpless, our practice of loving kindness, that brands us in the eyes of many of our opponents."

While services to the sick, the poor, and the unfortunate, which were initiated and for long undertaken by the Church, are now to a large extent provided by the State, there remains, and will always remain, an extensive and important sphere for the specifically Christian ministry. The needs of the outcasts, whom society despises and rejects, and of neglected classes whose wants most people are too preoccupied with their own concerns to perceive and remember, will always make a claim on Christian charity. Even among those for whom adequate material provision is made by the State there exist a multitude of individual needs which no large-scale administrative system can reach, and above all the need for personal understanding, sympathy, and friendship which no organi-

[1] Vol. 1, pp. 147 ff.

zation can supply, but must always be the gift of man to man.

The service of the Church is rendered to men. But it is not the world of which the Church is the servant. It can serve the world only as it is free from bondage to the world. The service which it renders is not a service of its own choosing, or that which the world desires, but that to which the Church is commissioned by Christ.

(c) *Witness*

The witness of the Church is to the manifestation of a new reality—the grace and truth that came by Jesus Christ—and to the coming Kingdom of God. It is directed not merely to individuals, in order that they may believe and be saved, but to the total life of the community. The beliefs and practices of society must be set in the light of the truth that has been revealed. The Church can fully serve men only as it helps them to see the whole of their life and all their activities in relation to the purpose of God. The Church has a responsibility to the community or nation as well as to the individual.

The manner in which the Church is called to discharge this function will vary with the circumstances of the age. The Church has different tasks to fulfil in different conditions of social and political life. Where it has been recently planted in a new soil, and is still young and small in numbers, its influence in the general life of the community is necessarily restricted. Its primary task is to win fresh adherents to the faith; though sometimes, as the history of the mission field shows, the freshness of its message and the contrast between it and the prevailing ideas enable the Church to exert an influence on the general thought and practice out of all proportion to its numbers. Sometimes, again, under autocratic and hostile

Governments severe restraints may be placed on the freedom of the Church. It may have to content itself with keeping alive the torch of faith in the hearts of a small handful of believers and waiting in patience for the day of God's deliverance. It may be compelled, as in the early centuries, to seek refuge in the catacombs. Under other conditions the Church may have full liberty to proclaim its own understanding of the truth and to express a judgment on public policy and social practice.

The question to which the mind of the Church must be addressed is the nature of the witness which is demanded from the Church to-day. Discussions of the task of the Church tend, under the influence of pre-war habits of thought, to presuppose a more or less stable state of society in which there may take place a slow and gradual permeation of Christian ideas. The question which the Churches must ask, if they want to come to grips with the realities of life to-day, is whether our customary conventional and comfortable ways of cultivating and expressing the religious life have any relevance to the earnestness of a revolutionary situation. The report of a Committee on the State of the Church submitted to the biennial meeting of the Federal Council of the Churches of Christ in America in December 1936[1] deplored "the widespread dependence of the Church upon secondary motives in maintaining the loyalty of its people." It is clear, the authors of the report say, that "many churches are depending too largely to-day upon the same motives which maintain clubs, lodges, and philanthropies. They feel that they must furnish novel attractions and entertainment and organized activities that will enable them to compete with secular organizations." That is plainly a trifling with the earnest issues of life that can make no appeal to the youth who to-day are seeking an end to

[1] Published in the *Christian Century* of December 30, 1936.

which they may wholly surrender their lives. But even when the Church keeps free from entanglement with matters extraneous to its proper mission, can we assure ourselves that its religious services do not degenerate too easily into occasions which awaken merely transient emotions, and provide a pleasing interlude in a week devoted to the real interests of life which remain unaffected by our worship? And in so far as this is true, can a Church which has so little pungency and provocation in its message expect to arrest or hold the attention of a generation, many of whose members are under the spell of the urge to death and are marching in their hundreds of thousands to imagined glory or extinction?

Belief in the Church and loyalty to it compel us to face these questions. On the answer given to them may depend whether there will continue to be a Church at all. In a time when the foundations of the world are moved, and men are peering anxiously into the future and asking themselves what direction they should take, the voice of the Church must be clear, definite, and challenging, if it is to receive serious attention. This does not mean the identification of the Church with a particular fashionable or unfashionable political programme or with any set of ideas derived from other sources than its own understanding of the truth by which it lives. A true word of prophecy must mean a response to God's call springing out of reflection on the Word committed to the Church. But if it is given to the Church to speak a prophetic word it will of necessity be a disturbing word. It will challenge and offend existing ideas, prejudices, and interest. We must not delude ourselves. It is not possible to have it both ways. In a world in which millions of men are prepared to fight and to die for their faith the Church may either count for very little, or it may count, by God's grace, for much—but only at a large cost. It may be God's purpose that the Church should regain a moral and spiritual leadership which it has largely lost. But if this is to come about the price must be paid in full. If we are not ready for this, we may as well resign ourselves to impotence. Men will rightly judge that the Christian faith is not a live alternative in the sphere of action.

CHAPTER VIII

THE NATURE OF THE CORPORATE LIFE

BEFORE we go on to consider, in the light of the survey
in Chapter VI, the action of Christians and of the Church
as an organized society in the social and political spheres,
it is desirable to recall to our minds some of the factors
which determine the nature of the corporate life. The
purpose of this chapter is not, of course, to present a
theory of society or to offer a systematic treatment of the
subject, but only to direct attention to certain features of
society of which account has to be taken in Christian
action.

I. THE ORGANIC ASPECT OF THE CORPORATE LIFE

The corporate life is at once something which men create
and something into which they are born. The fact that a
man cannot choose or exchange his parents illustrates
the truth that the corporate life is made up in part of
facts which are already given wholly independently of
the will of the individual. The family is a primordial fact
from which a man cannot free himself, a fact which
carries and conditions his whole existence. From his
parents he inherits certain physical and mental characteristics. He also acquires from them, and from the environment into which he is born, a certain outlook on life.
Through his family, neighbourhood, and nation he is the
heir of a particular cultural tradition. He participates in
the life of a particular people and in its historical experiences. To reflect on these facts is to realize how far
removed from reality is any view which thinks of life in
terms only of individuals. The life of the individual is

inextricably rooted in a biological and historical context which in a thousand ways conditions and influences his whole existence. These organic solidarities which are the basis of human existence have a profound significance for the development of the moral and Christian life. For the Christian they are the creation of divine Providence for the purpose of helping and supporting his moral growth, and the divinely appointed sphere in which he is called to serve God. Through participation in them he is involved in a network of responsibilities and obligations, the fulfilment of which ministers to his growth as a person. These organic bonds, however, are not only the natural soil in which the moral life may grow. They may also be a limiting factor and interpose obstacles to its growth. Here is found one of the great paradoxes of the corporate life. The claims of these natural solidarities have in the name of a higher loyalty both to be acknowledged and on occasion also denied.

2. THE PURSUIT OF COMMON PURPOSES

A second distinctive feature of the common life is that men, in virtue of their rational and social nature, are associated in an endless variety of ways for the achievement of common purposes. Co-operation in the pursuit of common ends is characteristic of the life of the family and of the nation with their biological foundations no less than of voluntary associations formed for specific purposes. An illuminating exposition of this aspect of the corporate life is given in Professor Barker's introductory essay in his translation of Gierke's *Natural Law and the Theory of Society*. Rejecting the view that associations are to be regarded as beings, or minds, or real persons, he finds the distinguishing mark of a group or association in a common and continuing purpose, "which permanently unites a number of individuals as the common content of their minds and the common intention of their wills."[1] This common purpose is not something immutable and invariable; it is something living, growing, and changing. All these various, partial, common purposes which constitute the being and unity of groups have to be related to the general common purpose of the State, and it is the distinctive function of the State to hold the balance between the conflicting purposes of groups and to see that they do not oppose or destroy the general common purpose of which it is the special trustee.[2]

This fact of association with others in carrying out the purposes by which the community maintains, expands, and enriches its own life gives rise to one of the main problems of which account has to be taken in considering Christian action in the corporate life. Where there is purpose there may be divergence of purpose. The purpose of the Christian is to carry out in all relations the will of God. But in every group of which he is a member, whether it be the nation or State, or a voluntary association, such as a trades union or employers' federation or an educational institution, he may be, and generally is, associated with those who do not share this Christian purpose. The group has a common purpose which is not identical with the Christian's purpose, but the realization of which, notwithstanding the imperfections of the process, is necessary for human existence or welfare. When this conflict of purposes arises, the Christian is confronted with the choice of withdrawing from an association, the purpose of which he feels to be incompatible with his Christian calling (which is possible in the case of a voluntary association but not as a rule in the case of the nation or the State), or of remaining a member of the association and seeking by protest, or by the quality of

[1] Page lxiii.   [2] Pages lxxix–lxxx.

his own action, to bring the common purpose into fuller accord with what he believes to be the will of God. For the solution of conflicts between contradictory purposes there can be no easy, general, or universally valid solution. Such conflicts are the stuff of life. They arise in an endless multiplicity of new and unrepeatable situations. There is no escape for the individual from the responsibility of decision. In these responsible choices life finds its meaning. The only thing that men take with them when the end comes is the character formed by their decisions.

Whatever else may have to be said about the corporate life, we must never allow ourselves to be carried too far from the solid truth on which Professor Barker insists, that groups, from the village or club to the State or nation, are essentially "organizations of persons, or schemes of personal relations . . . constructed by the thought of persons, consisting in the thought of persons, sustained by the thought of persons and revised (or even destroyed) by the thought of persons."[1] It is necessary to ask, however, whether corporate life does not also contain complicating factors that lie outside the sphere of deliberate purpose.

3. THE LAWS OF THINGS

Men can achieve their purposes, whether individual or common, only through the use of things. Even when they seek to serve one another as persons they have to use things as a means of rendering the service. The things which are instrumental to human purpose are governed by their own laws. Material things and their laws are a limiting factor in all human action. The dialectical materialism of Karl Marx is the assertion, though in an exaggerated and onesided way, of an important truth,

[1] Pages xvi–xvii.

in its insistence on the extent to which men's ideas and behaviour are conditioned by their material environment. Christian action in the corporate life, like all other action, has to take account of the nature of reality. The Christian scientist has to express his Christianity in being a good scientist. What society rightly expects of the Christian engineer is not that he should exhibit exemplary piety apart from his profession, but that he should be a competent and efficient engineer. The Christian who expresses an opinion about the relation of Christian principles to the economic system must be prepared, even at the cost of many a bad headache, to master the facts of the economic system. The patient study of, and humble submission to, the laws of things is one expression of the Christian's trust in God, who ordered the world as it is; at the same time it is a divinely appointed discipline for the human spirit which deepens, educates, and enriches the spiritual life.

4. THE LAWS OF INSTITUTIONS

Not only things but human institutions are subject to laws of their own, which have to be understood and respected. These institutions, constituted by persons for the achievement of their purposes, are not only subject to natural conditions which control their working but tend to acquire a momentum and energy of their own.

The economic system, for example, is the result of a multitude of individual purposes acting on the material resources, and with the instruments, available at a given period. But no one can say that the results of the existing system were consciously and deliberately willed by anyone. It is only too evident that man has become enslaved by forces which his own purposes have brought into existence. Men may often have to act in a way entirely contrary to

that which they would wish in order to maintain in operation a system which human purposes have brought into
existence, the immediate collapse of which would spell
disaster for society. There arises a fundamental and inescapable conflict of responsibilities, in which men can fulfil
their duty to society in one respect only by violating their
obligations to it in another. A company may do things in
the interests of its shareholders which its directors might
hesitate to do as individuals, and it may refrain, and
ought often to refrain, from doing things which individuals
are free to do. There is found in modern society, as Sir
Josiah Stamp has said, "the complication, insignificant in
the time of Christ, of group relations, where ethical
judgment is made on behalf of the individual in some
delegated area of his rights without engaging his whole
ethical personality."[1]

It is impossible to exaggerate the fundamental change
which is taking place in the conditions of human life
through the multiplication and intensification of group
activities which science and technical invention have
brought about. We may agree with Professor Barker in
refusing to regard groups as persons, or to ascribe to them
a real mind independent of the minds of the persons
composing them. But the association of persons in common
activities, whether in a business enterprise, or in cultural
pursuits, or in the community of a nation, establishes in
the course of time a tradition, accumulates recognized
principles of action, and creates a spirit which impose
themselves on all members of the group and which can
be changed only by a long, slow, and gradual process.
Forms of conduct become habitual and once established
operate in society as forces independent of the conscious
choices of individuals. It may be true that moral responsibility (as distinct from legal responsibility) cannot be

[1] *Motive and Method in a Christian Order*, p. 41.

attached to a group. But in so far as this is true, it follows that society, confronted with the unceasing growth of group life, if it is not to suffer spiritual disintegration, must address itself to the immense task of discovering the real centres of responsibility in group activities and of creating in the members of groups the sense of moral responsibility for their common activities.

It need not surprise us that the question is asked by serious minds whether the Christian ethic, with its emphasis on the direct responsibility of persons towards other persons, is adequate to meet the needs of modern society. Even if the Church were to be wholly loyal to its faith and fully to discharge its functions, it is urged, this would not suffice for the needs of modern society. "Neither the cardinal virtues of the Greeks," it is maintained in a recent work, "nor the Christian virtues of faith, hope, and charity, nor yet the fruits of the Spirit, outlined by St. Paul, such as meekness, gentleness, longsuffering, and so forth, are able to establish themselves as the essentially vital attitudes which it is necessary to adopt in order to live fully and adequately, and to meet the demands which life makes upon men. The dwindling private relationships of men call for these, but not the work of the world."[1] Speaking out of an exceptionally wide experience of industrial and public life, Sir Josiah Stamp urges that "the whole body of ethics needs to be recast in the mould of modern corporate relations."[2]

5. THE NATION AND THE STATE

A discussion of the problems of the nation and the State does not belong to this volume. The profound complications to which they give rise in human relations must,

---

[1] E. E. Thomas, *A Prelude to Religion*, pp. 248-9.
[2] *Motive and Method in a Christian Order*, p. 41.

however, be clearly in our minds in the consideration of Christian action in the corporate life.

In this field the conflict between the principles which should govern the relations of persons with other persons and the necessities of public action reaches its most acute point. The nation and the State are custodians of an historic life, of traditions and institutions which have grown through a long period of time. They have the responsibilities of trustees. The State has to act on behalf of the community as a whole; consequently it has to be guided by the general sentiment and not by ideals which may be cherished by a small minority of the community. As things are at present the nation and State are not subject, like the individual, to a higher authority or to the reign of law, nor does there exist any living consciousness of community between different peoples on which a world order might be based. Therefore the affairs of states have to be guided by quite other principles than those which regulate the conduct of individuals in their relations with other individuals. The problem is forcibly stated in the following passage from the *Life of Archbishop Magee*:

"It was to him perfectly clear that a state could not continue to exist on the condition of carrying out all Christian precepts for the individual, and their Lord said so. He said, 'My kingdom is not of this world.' It was, therefore, a huge mistake to attempt to turn His kingdom into a kingdom of this world, or to turn the kingdoms of the world into His kingdom. Again, he thought they could not speak of the State as if it was an individual and apply all the maxims of individual ethics absolutely to it. The State was not an individual. It was a trustee for a great many individuals. . . . The great law of the Church of Christ was self-sacrifice, and the motive power of that law was love. The principle of the State was justice, and the motive power of the State was force, and that was the essential difference between the two."[1]

When Professor Barker finds the essence of the State in a purpose of law,[2] he is emphasizing only one side of the ambiguous entity of the State. There is in the State also a natural, non-rational element—the brute fact of power. Might is inseparable from the existence of the State. It belongs to its nature to use force both in self-defence against external enemies and as a means of controlling its own members. Even when force is not exercised it is always present in the background as a resource to which appeal may be made when occasion requires. Between the coercion which is inseparable from political life and the Christian law of love there is an insurmountable tension.

6. THE SOURCES OF SOCIAL EVIL

Professor John Bennett, in an enlightening paper contributed to the volume on *The Christian Faith and the Common Life*, has called attention to the variety and multiplicity of the sources of social evil. He utters a needed warning against the temptation unduly to simplify the problem. Action in the social and political field is conditioned to-day by the scale of social organization and by the rapidity of change. Men's faculties of sight and hearing are no greater than they were when civilization began. Their minds and memories have not increased in capacity. The working day has not grown in length. Yet with these continuing limitations men have to deal with problems which owing to the increase of scale have become different not merely in degree but in kind. Again, the pace of development has become so rapid that situations change

---

[1] *Life of Archbishop Magee*, vol. ii, 276, quoted by the Bishop of Durham in *Christian Morality*, p. 254.

[2] *Natural Law and the Theory of Society*, p. lxxxvii.

far more swiftly than the patterns of thought with which men try to meet them. The situation has become so complex that it is impossible to foresee the results of any action; this state of affairs leaves men bewildered and paralysed. Even where goodwill is present men do not know how to translate it into action.

The evils of society are the result not only of human sin but also of human finitude. Vast and terrible as are men's crimes, deep and pitiful as are their moral lethargy and spiritual torpor, there are evils in society for which no one can be held morally responsible. Nature, M. Bergson tells us,[1] has willed that men should have a social life, but also that it should be limited in range. Men have been created with small-scale minds. The range of their imagination, the compass of their interests are restricted. These badges of their finitude limit the good which they are often disposed to do. Ill-health, lack of physical fitness, fatigue, the effects of age with its hardening of the mind, the specialization of modern society, by which men become so immersed in a particular task that they have no leisure or energy to think in wider terms, the crust of prejudices, the emotional maladjustments from which as the result of a defective education in home and school the majority of men suffer in greater or less degree—these and many other factors, enumerated by Professor Bennett, combining in an infinite variety of subtle ways with human egoism, pride, and moral weakness, are among the obstacles that have to be surmounted in any attempt to improve society. Programmes of social reform are sometimes put forward which would require for their realization the re-education of the entire community. Before they could be carried out the prevailing patterns of thought and feeling would need to be wholly changed.

[1] *Les deux Sources de la Morale et de la Religion*, Chapter I.

When we turn to the moral evil in society which it is the special concern of the Church to combat, there opens up a question on which Christian thought is divided, but which involves issues too important and far-reaching to be ignored.

There are those who would attribute the evils of society wholly to human ignorance and the perversity of human wills.

> In tragic life, God wot,
> No villains need be. Passions spin the plot.
> We are betrayed by what is false within.

Even if this be true, the evil which is in men's hearts and thoughts permeates and infects the whole social order. It gathers force through its collective expression. It embodies itself in false philosophies of life which dominate the whole temper of an age and in perverted relations between men which issue in deepening hatred, distrust, and conflict.

There are others, however, to whom it appears that evil has a deeper source. They detect in the universe a destructive or demonic principle operating beyond the range of human volition; or they accept the Biblical view of the existence of a superhuman evil will or wills.

Confronted with the breaking forth of repressed elements in our civilization and of wild and untamed forces, and equipped with the new knowledge of human nature provided by analytical psychology, men are more fully aware to-day than previously of the dark, irrational forces which surround and underlie human existence. Man is less secure in his control of things than former generations were disposed to believe. Human personality does not sit enthroned above the conflict directing its course, but may itself become the plaything of hidden powers. "We can no longer deny," writes Professor C. G.

Jung, "that the dark stirrings of the unconscious are effective powers—that psychic forces exist which cannot, for the present at least, be fitted in with our rational world-order."[1] There is a deepened awareness of the powerful, hidden, nameless forces on which human life is borne as on a tide and out of which consciousness arises, to illuminate, as some would say, for a brief moment, like a flickering candle, the surrounding darkness. In contrast with the view of human reason as independent of race or history or economic circumstances, men are aware to-day how profoundly its exercise is influenced by all these factors. The irrational, hidden forces which modern psychology has revealed in the individual life underlie the whole of human existence. To ignore these unfathomable forces is to fail to understand the tragic nature of human existence.

The consciousness of conflict with superhuman forces of evil cannot easily be eliminated from the Bible or from the life of Christ. Professor Heim has recently reminded us[2] how fundamental in the life of Jesus was the conflict with satanic powers. His whole ministry was a continuous war with the forces of evil. His death was not simply the result of a struggle between competing ideas or views of life, but the final, terrible, decisive battle against an evil will that was set on defeating the purpose of God. When divine goodness became incarnate, the one in whom it was embodied was rejected and crucified.

The issue has been raised because the view we take of the nature of evil in the universe must profoundly affect our understanding of the Christian action that is demanded in the corporate life. If we believe the primary source of evil to lie in the ignorance and perversity of men, we may hope by a process of education and

---

[1] *Modern Man in Search of a Soul*, p. 234.
[2] *Jesus der Herr*, pp. 104–5, 111–13.

enlightenment progressively to mitigate the evils from which society is suffering. But if we have to war against a destructive principle in the universe itself and against superhuman powers of evil, the struggle assumes a grimmer and sterner aspect. We cannot in our own strength contend successfully against satanic powers. The fellowship of the Church gains a new and deepened meaning, since only in the might of that fellowship and of the divine redemption which is its source can we become victors over all the powers of darkness.

CHAPTER IX

THE WITNESS AND ACTION OF THE CHURCH IN THE CORPORATE LIFE

I. THE NECESSITY OF THE EXPRESSION OF CHRISTIAN FAITH IN THE CORPORATE LIFE

CHRISTIAN faith must express itself in the corporate life. There is no other sphere in which it can express itself. Christians, like other men, are members of society. They participate in the activities of the common life. The ways of serving God in the world are infinite in variety, but none are unrelated to the common life. To live is to act, and action is invariably conditioned in greater or less degree by the prevailing practice, customs, and institutions of society.

It is not surprising that in face of the complexities of the corporate life Christians should be tempted to make a separation between the sphere of public action and the inner life of the soul. The corporate life appears to be dominated by forces that are irreconcilable with the Christian spirit of love. But to turn aside from the activities and struggles of common men is an evasion of Christian responsibility. The Christian is called to fulfil God's will, not in some remote and future world, but here and now in relation to the reality which encompasses, challenges, and resists us. Faith in God is real only as it confronts the particulars of history. Only by acting in accordance with God's will in the concrete historical situation in which He has placed us can we, in the full reality of our being, enter into fellowship with God. As Professor Brunner has written, retreat from the actual world would mean that "real action would be entirely withdrawn from the influence of the Christian ethic. It is *here*, in this border-land between technical action and ethics—in economics, in politics, in public life—that the great decisions are made. If the Christian ethic fails at this point, it fails all along the line."[1]

This insistence is all the more necessary in face of the modern attack on Christianity. It is a vital matter that the Church should open its mind to the full force of this attack. The essence of religion, it is maintained, is the creation of an ideal and imaginary world, which offers consolation for the inevitable frustrations of life. By so doing it diverts men's minds from the struggle in which the reality of human life consists—the struggle to create freedom and community in the world, not of idea, but of fact. Religion is inimical to man's true welfare since it offers him an unreal consolation for material injustices and provides him with an escape from the struggles of society. It is not a sufficient answer to these charges to say that Christianity is concerned with other and higher goods than those which men are seeking. For the sting of the attack is that the cultivation of the religious life of the individual instead of identifying him more deeply with other men in their struggle and need detaches him from the common lot. If that charge can be driven home Christianity will have been betrayed by its own professors. For it will mean that Christianity has nothing to do with the concrete experiences and open conflicts of life, and consequently is without importance for the life which men actually have to live.

2. THE CHURCH AS AN ORGANIZED SOCIETY AND AS A COMMUNITY LIVING IN THE WORLD

The starting-point of a discussion of the witness and action of the Church in the corporate life must be the far-

[1] *The Divine Imperative*, p. 262.

reaching distinction made in an earlier chapter[1] between the Church as a society organized for worship and the preaching of the Word and the Church as a community of men and women living in the world but committed through faith in Christ to a new outlook on life and a new way of living. The witness and action of the Church as an organized society, and as such distinct and separate from other forms of human association, and the witness and action of the Church through its individual members who at the same time in an endless variety of callings participate in the activities of these other associations, are two entirely distinct, though intimately related, questions. Much confusion of thought has resulted from failure clearly to distinguish them. Although both forms of witness and action are essential, and although the two are inseparably connected, as a rule, in discussing the witness and action of the Church in the corporate life, we tend to think of what can be done by the Church acting in its corporate capacity, whereas, in fact, what can be accomplished by lay men and women actively engaged from day to day in the affairs of the world is incomparably greater in its range, effectiveness, and importance. The Church as an organized society stands outside the activities of the social and political life. The Christian laity participate in these activities. Transformation from within is immeasurably more effective than any influence that can be brought to bear from without.

In the present chapter we shall examine this influence from within, exercised through the lives of Christian men and women, reserving for the next chapter the consideration of the witness and action of the Church as an organized society. But while it is important for the purpose of discussion, and in order that matters of vital importance may not be overlooked, to distinguish these

[1] Pages 156 ff.

two forms of action, they belong inseparably together and have their springs in a common life. It is the one indivisible Church which expresses its life both in its corporate action and in the lives of its individual members.

It may seem to some that if this is what is meant it would be simpler and clearer, in the title and text of this chapter, to speak of the witness and action of Christians rather than of the witness and action of the Church. But this change would cut at the root of the whole argument. The point on which we wish most of all to insist is that Christian action in the corporate life, though it is the action of individuals, does not mean isolated action but action by Christians as members of the Church. It is action springing out of the reality of the Christian fellowship, rooted in obedience to the Word which the Church proclaims, inspired and guided by its ministries, supported by its prayers, and examined and tested in intercourse with other Christians. It is with the Church as a divine society that we are concerned in this chapter as much as in the chapter which follows. But while there we shall be dealing with the Church acting through its official representatives our present concern is with the manifestation of the life of the Church in the whole body of its members.

3. THE WITNESS AND ACTION OF THE CHRISTIAN LAITY

The distinction which we have emphasized coincides, not entirely but in part, with the distinction between the functions of the clergy or Christian ministry and the responsibilities of the lay members of the Church.

The basis of our argument is that Christian faith can be a transforming and creative force in the corporate life only to the extent in which it takes possession of the minds of multitudes of lay men and women and provides the principles by which their conduct in private and public life are determined. There are, of course, already large numbers of lay men and women, who are loyal members of the Church and who by the integrity and unselfishness of their lives offer a convincing witness to the faith which they profess. Such lives are the salt of society.

But when we consider how this Christian lay activity may be greatly multiplied we are confronted by problems which call for the most serious attention. As has already been pointed out,[1] there is a far wider gap than there ought to be between the Church as an organized society and the lay world. There are many lay men and women who are conscious of religious need, who in their secret hearts long for the help that they feel that the Church might give them, but who do not find that the Church satisfies that need. It is not a real solution of this problem to say that the fault lies in such people themselves; that they are closing their hearts to the Christian message and that the Church must just go on trying to convert them. It is at least possible that the fault is to be found equally in our own presentation of the gospel and in its expression in the present institutional forms of the Church. We have neither seen the problem, nor is there any hope of solving it, if we assume, as we are too apt to do, that what is wanted is mainly that we should redouble our energies to persuade people to come to Church and to contribute more liberally to Church funds or to take a hand in Church work. All this is right and necessary, but it is to attack the problem only from one side. It has to be attacked from both sides, if a real solution is to be found. It may be that the Church in its present institutional form is not adapted to the real needs of the lay world.

If the gap is to be bridged, new methods must be

[1] Pages 107 ff.

devised for getting into touch with lay men and women other than inviting them to participate in the present services and activities of the Church. There must be a coming together of churchmen and those who are distrustful of the Church, not on the basis, expressed or implied, that those outside must repent (though the necessity of repentance on the part of all concerned is not in question) and return to the fold of their fathers, but on a basis of equal and frank discussion and a common readiness to learn. Beginnings have been made in this direction, as, for example (to take only one illustration which happens to be within my own knowledge) in weekend gatherings arranged by some Anglican bishops for laymen in their dioceses. But if the gap is as wide and serious as it appears to be, the task of restoring connections between the preaching, teaching, and institutional activities of the Church and the life of our time demands the adoption of new methods on a vastly increased scale. If it is to be undertaken successfully it will certainly require the development of new types of ministry, including probably lay ministries. The vital matter is that, in addition to present forms of ministry (the necessity for which is not in question), approaches to the lay world need to be devised, not on the assumption that the Church is all right and that those who hold aloof from it are wrong, but on the basis that the question is open whether churchmen may not be far wrong and that many things in the Church may need to be changed.

That is, however, only one side, though an immensely important side, of the problem. It is essential that in attempting to deal with it we should never forget that our concern from first to last is with the rule of God and not with the laity just because they are lay. In insisting that there is need to discuss with those outside the Church on a basis of complete equality, and with a deep humility and readiness to learn what they feel to be lacking or amiss in its ministries, we do not for a moment mean that the ideas and desires of the natural man have any say in determining the nature of the Church. Christ is the one and only Head of any Church that is entitled to be called Christian. There is no suggestion that those who have never given their loyalty to Christ or been converted to the Christian understanding of life should transform the Church into a cultural association or philanthropic society or something other than the Church of Christ. That would mean not the reformation but the end of the Church. When we speak of action by the laity, we mean always and only specifically Christian action. It is the action of those who acknowledge allegiance to Christ and who are growing in an understanding of the obligations of the Christian life.

4. LINES OF ADVANCE

If the problem is to be taken effectively in hand, advance must be made in three main directions.

In the first place the attempt must be made to relate the spiritual and pastoral ministries of the Church more directly and intimately to the specific tasks of the common life. Large congregational services cannot enter with sufficient fullness and in sufficient detail into the problems which specially concern individuals or particular groups. If the wide gulf which exists in the modern world between work and worship is to be bridged we have to discover means by which the actualities of daily life are lifted up into worship and the common round of activities is sanctified and fortified by prayer. Endeavours to meet the needs of special groups are, of course, not lacking in the present ministries of the Church. But much fresh, creative thought needs to be given to the problem, and new experiments are needed in many directions. There may be room, for example, for a large extension of the movement to provide retreats for lay men and women, in which they can face the problems and occupations of their lives in an atmosphere of worship. As the best means of meeting the need is discovered, new types of ministry will be required to supplement the present parochial and congregational ministries.

Secondly, there is need for much more definite ethical guidance. In the baffling complexities of life to-day it is extraordinarily difficult for the individual Christian to know what Christian loyalty demands in practical conduct. It is impossible for him alone and unaided to think his way through the problems, and if he is left without help it is not surprising if he loses heart and acquiesces resignedly in the prevailing standards and practices of society. The view which would lay the whole burden of responsibility on the individual to discover in each concrete situation what is God's will is a heroic but unreal conception. The individual Christian needs the guidance and support of the Christian society. While the Church has a body of fairly clear and definite teaching in regard to Christian obligations in the sphere of personal relationships (though even in this field there is urgent need for fresh and constructive thought in many directions), it has little authoritative guidance to offer about what is right or wrong in the sphere of public conduct.

Help towards a clearer understanding of the ethical implications of the gospel must come in part from thinkers and scholars. But indispensable as is their contribution, it is no less essential that groups of Christians should associate themselves in seeking light and mutual support in dealing with the problems that are their special and immediate concern. A third important line of advance, therefore, is the multiplication of small groups of Christians for the purpose of mutual help in Christian witness and action.

These groups may be local, having as their primary concern the social evils of a particular town or rural area. Their objects may be primarily spiritual, i.e. to sustain and fortify through prayer and fellowship those who seek to advance the cause of righteousness, to relieve distress and to serve the common good in various forms of public activity. Or the groups may have a specific social objective of putting an end to some local injustice or meeting some local need. No Christian congregation can escape its responsibilities to its immediate neighbourhood. If through the faithful preaching of the Gospel men and women commit themselves to war against the devil and all his works, the first duty is to find out what injustices there are to be removed and what miseries and want to be relieved in the immediate neighbourhood. The life of the Church would be revitalized if in every parish or congregation there were groups of Christian men and women banded together for this purpose, and developing through the discipline of the conflict with social evil a growingly sensitive Christian conscience.

Other groups may have a predominantly professional character. This suggestion has been put forward by Dr. Ernest Johnson. "The possibilities of religious education on the adult level," he writes, "have scarcely been touched. It would seem to need no argument that a religious communion entertaining definite social ideals and acknowledging an educational responsibility should have a programme for every functional group within its membership. . . . If religious education is to become significant with reference to the ethical standards of the adult generation, it must make provision for the study by functional groups—lawyers, physicians, engineers, teachers, labour leaders, bankers, and many others—of the ideals of the religion to which they claim allegiance in their bearing upon vocational tasks."[1] A similar suggestion has been made in a paper from Germany, where small but promising experiments have been made in this direction.

Wherever there has been a revival of Christianity of an enduring kind it has generally found expression in the spontaneous activity of small groups meeting for mutual encouragement, fellowship, and common effort. The conception of "cells" is wholly congruous with the genius of Christianity. May not the formation of such cells of Christian witness and service be the distinctive Christian contribution to the social and political struggles of our time? To be effectively changed a social system must be changed from within and in all its parts. This leaves entirely open the question at what stage a radical change of the whole system is required in order to allow the new, constructive forces the opportunity of further expansion. But to make an outward change of system while the mind remains unconverted and the old habits persist can result only in disillusionment. The existing evils will merely assume another form. The only order which can be a really better order is one in which there is a greater sense of responsibility of men towards men, and that responsibility is something that grows through exercise and must be learned and practised in lesser spheres before it can be effectively exercised in wider fields. It has to be learned first in the family, in the neighbourhood, in local government, in professional associations, in various social groupings. It is unrealistic to suppose that a nation can order successfully its political and economic life in the national sphere unless it can call to its service persons who have been trained to civic responsibility in these more restricted fields of service. If we try to envisage a

[1] *The Church and Society*, pp. 205–6.

Church fully alive to its responsibilities in the social and political spheres, ought not the picture in our minds to be one of the growth of a multitude of centres of spontaneous activity in which Christians associate themselves to bear the Christian witness in their neighbourhood or profession, to war against evil where they encounter it in daily life and in the immediate environment which is in some measure under their control? In proportion as such groups increased there would arise a force in the life of a people capable of transforming its institutions and of bringing about a true revolution.

5. THE CONTRIBUTION OF THE CHRISTIAN MINISTRY

To advance along the lines suggested the Christian ministry have an indispensable contribution to make.

It is their privilege as ministers of the Word and sacraments to bring to the witness and service of Christian men and women actively engaged in the affairs of the world the re-enforcement, enlargement, and discipline of Christian worship. It is not necessary to add to what has already been said on this subject.[1]

The immense task confronts the Church in our day of relating Christian preaching and teaching more directly to the thought and experiences of the common life. Too often the presentation of the Christian message is couched in traditional and conventional phraseology which conveys little or no meaning to the ordinary man. It is not merely a question of language but of the whole approach to religious questions. If this difficulty is to be overcome it is necessary that Christian ministers should set themselves deliberately to learn as well as to teach. From the laity may be learned lessons of life that find no place in the curriculum of the theological college.

[1] Pages 156 ff.

This is easy to concede in theory but difficult to carry out in practice. The laity are shy and reserved in the presence of the clergy. There is a traditional relationship of teacher and taught, pastor and flock, that stands in the way of intercourse on a basis of complete equality. Only by a resolute effort of the will and by the humility which is born of prayer, can the barrier be broken down and conditions created in which the minister may be learner as well as teacher. Opportunities may offer, or may be made, of participation in groups of representatives of various walks of life, in which the problems of individual responsibility in industry, in the professions and in social betterment are freely discussed, and in which the minister claims no initiative but takes part, not as one who already possesses the answer or the final truth, but on a footing of equality as a man among men.

Reference has already been made, and will be made further, to the need for ethical guidance. The extent to which such new insights as may be gained permeate the whole Christian body and lead to fruitful action will depend in a large degree on the teaching of the ordinary ministry. More systematic provision needs to be made for the ethical education of the laity and in particular of the young. Several American correspondents have drawn attention to the wide differences of outlook which tend to prevail in the United States between pulpit and pew in regard to standards of social obligation. Preaching and teaching ought to include explicit and continuous instruction in regard to the social relevance of the Christian faith. It is necessary to draw out the inexhaustible wealth of meaning in the essential values that are implied in the Christian understanding of life—the infinite value of men for whom Christ died, the sacredness of personality, the claim of every child to have the opportunity of bringing to the largest fruition what is in him, the dangers of wealth, to which the Gospels so frequently recur, the responsibility of men for one another's lives. To this teaching point may be given by showing the extent to which it is denied and contradicted by existing conditions. The facts about the present social system have to be brought home to the imagination. The teachings of the New Testament become alive only when their connection is clearly seen with the actual life of to-day. People need to be helped to see through the rationalizations by which they hide from themselves the true facts and to understand the extent to which their opinions and attitudes are determined by the interests of the social group to which they belong.

It is impossible to rate too highly the opportunities of the evangelistic, teaching, and pastoral work of the Christian ministry. In the parish and congregation are the lay men and women who by their witness and action can bring about profound transformations in the social life. In it also are the young, who will carry the public responsibilities of the future. Whatever changes may be needed in institutions, it is certain that these changes will accomplish little unless they are accompanied by changes in the men and women who have to work them. There cannot be a better society apart from better men and women. "How to break the vicious circle," writes a distinguished economist, holding liberal and advanced views, in a paper contributed to the preparatory work for the Conference, "that you will not have better men without a better society, and that you can only get a better society, if at any rate an important minority has reached a higher standard of conduct, this is the crucial point in all our discussions." In urging that the supreme concern of the Christian ministry is with the making of better men and women we are not advocating an individualistic Gospel. What we envisage is poles removed from the concentration of interest on the saving of individual souls. It is that a Church aflame with social passion should recognize that the largest contribution of the Christian ministry to social transformation is an indirect one, and that the awakening, education, and spiritual encouragement of those who bear the varied responsibilities of the corporate life is the highest and most rewarding strategy.

What has been said has been written in full awareness of the multiplicity of burdens which the Christian minister has to-day to carry. The variety of demands on him leave little leisure for fresh tasks. If these are to be undertaken, it will be necessary for some to find a means of emancipating themselves from the bondage of the machine and to subordinate claims of secondary importance to what requires most urgently to be done. If large progress is to be made, however, the necessity will arise of setting aside specially prepared men to undertake new forms of service.

6. A NEW ORIENTATION

Our plea in this chapter is for a fresh orientation and a new perspective in our thought about the witness and action of the Church in the corporate life. As will be plain from what is said in the following chapter, there is no intention of belittling the witness of the Church in its corporate capacity in public affairs. Without this reinforcement the witness of individual Christians will lack a proper setting and in consequence will lose much of its efficacy. But since the transformation of social life must be brought about, not by influence exerted from without, but by forces working from within, we misconceive the task of the Church in the social sphere when we think of it primarily and mainly in terms of action by the Church as an organized society.

It is the members of the Church, who discharge the responsibilities of the common life in a countless variety of occupations and in an infinite multiplicity of daily acts and decisions, that are the leaven which leavens the whole lump. In this faithful, silent witness they are fulfilling the priestly function of the Church. They permeate with the spirit of Christian love the varied relations of men with one another and make them kindlier, humaner, and more wholesome. By their understanding of the true ends of life they unobtrusively criticize the standards of society and subtly change the attitude of their fellows. By performing their tasks in dependence on God and in the spirit of worship, they redeem the social life from the aridity and shallowness of secularism. These are what William James described as the "invisible molecular moral forces that work from individual to individual, stealing in through the crannies of the world like so many soft rootlets, or like the capillary oozing of water, and yet rending the hardest monuments of man's pride, if you give them time."[1]

Christian action which springs from the central Christian motive and which estimates right and wrong in the light of Christ has its own peculiar perspective in which it views and judges all things. This perspective does not lead to any uniformity of outlook on, or attitude towards, the many-coloured, many-sided, changing panorama of life. Differences of insight, of experience and of historical circumstances give rise among Christians not merely to divergent but also to conflicting views, ideals, and programmes. There is no single Christian ideal for society which Christians can unitedly offer to the world, and for which the support of those who are not Christians can be claimed. But in spite of these differences of outlook and ideal, the attitude of Christians, since it is

[1] *Letters of William James*, vol. ii, p. 90.

prompted by the Christian motive and inspired by values different from those prevailing in society, acts as a leaven. It is an indisputable historical fact that the Christian judgment of the ideals and practices of society has had a far-reaching influence on the secular life and brought about changes in its standards and values.

In the conditions of to-day in particular, where the direct action and influence of the Church is in many quarters restricted or disregarded, an exceptional importance attaches to this indirect influence through the lives and attitudes of individuals on the prevailing cultural ideals and the unconsciously and instinctively accepted values that determine the life of a particular age. Even when Christianity is openly repudiated and the corporate life is governed by entirely other principles there still remains the possibility through this indirect influence of giving sociological expression to Christian motives and points of view. Programmes which Christians are prompted by their understanding of life to recommend or support may be accepted by those who are not Christians as sound and wise. In this way a scarcely noticed but profound influence may be brought to bear on the whole social order. It is true that there cannot be a Christian social order, or a Christian world order, unless it is composed of Christian men and women. But it may mean much that the standards and ideals of an age should be influenced in such a way as to create a better atmosphere and a more favourable environment for Christian life, that injustices and social evils should progressively be remedied, and that a new spirit should be infused into politics, industry, education, and other social activities.

If the spread of this leaven be our primary aim there must be a re-orientation of the thought and of the present activities of the Church directed to the achievement of this end. The life of the Church revolves round two poles. The one is the Gospel, with which it has been put in trust. The other is the world which needs to be saved. The activity of the Church must always be rooted in, and proceed from, the first. But there is always the danger of our losing touch with the second. If to a large extent this has actually happened in the modern world, it may be the task of our generation, taking for this purpose a firmer hold of the Gospel, to direct its main energies to restoring the severed connection.

In his recent book, *God and the Common Life*, Professor R. L. Calhoun has suggested that the root cause of the present evil and distress in the world is found in the divorce between work and worship. Where religion is not rooted in the day's work and the yearly round, there takes place a fragmentation of life and the sterilization of both the severed parts. "A secularized, self-centred daily life, on the one hand, and formalized, pious occasions, on the other, become scarred fragments which neither taken separately nor added together can be a living whole." It is precisely with such disjointed members of secularized work and detached worship that we have to deal in the modern world.

If this be our real problem, then the obligation resting on us is to refuse to be content with the present ministries of the Church which proceed, as they must do, from the one centre but fail to make sufficient contact with the other. Instead of pressing people to avail themselves of these ministries, the Church must have at least some adventurers who by a bold leap will take their stand on the other side of the gulf and find a starting point for their ministry in the needs and activities of the common life. An effort must be made to discover the kind of help and ministry that men and women need to strengthen them in the actual conflicts of life and to illuminate their tasks. Such an effort, if successful, is bound to lead in countless ways that cannot now be foreseen to a fresh, and immensely fruitful, re-orientation and re-organization of the life and activities of the Church.

CHAPTER X

THE WITNESS AND ACTION OF THE CHURCH AS AN ORGANIZED SOCIETY

WE may now turn to the witness and action of the Church as an organized society in the corporate life. By this we mean the action of the Church through its ecclesiastical heads and leaders, through its synods, councils and assemblies and other official organs, and through the clergy and ministers, who are its office-bearers.

I. THE WITNESS OF THE CHURCH REGARDING THE PURPOSE OF MAN'S EXISTENCE

The primary responsibility of the Church to society is to bear public witness to the truth about the meaning and purpose of life as revealed in Christ. In considering what this means in practice, we shall do well to remind ourselves again that what the Church has to proclaim is not a law or a set of ideals but a Gospel. It is this message of divine redemption that sets men free from bondage to the world to serve God in the world as His sons. In the fulfilment of this ministry the Church is calling into existence forces which must have a transforming influence on the social order.

It has to be remembered, further, that the Gospel which the Church has to proclaim is not merely a Gospel for the individual but a Gospel of redemption for the world. The Christian faith is that the coming of Christ has brought about a fundamental change in the relation of man to God and has initiated a new epoch in human history.

It is the principles of this new order into which men

may be redeemed that the Church has to proclaim. There is no reason to suppose that the Church can offer any helpful advice as to how the affairs of the world should be conducted on the assumptions of the old, unregenerate order.

It is the task of the Church to remind men of the true end and aim of their existence. It brings to them an assurance of the value and dignity of man as the object of God's love. In face of the widespread devaluation of man to-day the Church has the high mission of recalling men to a sense of the potentialities of their being. In a world in which life seems cheap, in which the individual often appears to be nothing more than a cog in a machine, and in which multitudes fritter away a trivial existence in a succession of new sensations and frivolous pleasures, men need to be saved from despair and an aimless existence by the reminder that they have been created for responsible self-hood as the children of God.

Moreover, in its Christian faith the Church possesses a true doctrine of community. As against every form of egoism and individualism, it believes and proclaims that those who are redeemed by God and called to His service are bound by an inescapable compulsion to the service of their fellow-men. Delivered from self-centredness, which is death, into a true existence in trust in God and love towards Him, they are impelled to express this love to God in love to men. They are bound in the love of God to an unlimited obligation to their fellows, and these bonds constitute true community. On the other hand the Christian conception of community as the free and self-giving response of persons to persons is equally opposed to any form of collectivism in which persons are subordinated to organization and the individual is sacrificed to the achievement of impersonal ends. The individual is not merely the instrument of social purposes but as the object of God's love he is an end in himself. There are objective values and purposes which society has to pursue in order to maintain itself, and in so far as these are necessary for the general good the tasks which they impose may be freely taken up by the individual into his will as a means by which his love to his neighbour may find expression and fulfilment. But for the Christian the true meaning and satisfaction of life are found in the dedication of his whole personal being to the service of a loving God and in relations of trust and responsibility, of love and friendship, between himself and his fellow-men.

2. THE ETHICAL IMPLICATIONS OF THE GOSPEL

The Gospel is not a code of morals or a new law. But the new mind which is formed in those who have responded to the revelation of a new reality in Christ must express itself in new forms of behaviour. It belongs to the prophetic and teaching office of the Church to expound the implications of the Christian understanding of life and to make clear the kind of behaviour to which belief in the Gospel prompts.

Such broad assertions as that Christians are bound to obey the law of love or to strive for social justice do not go far towards helping the individual to know what he ought to do in particular cases. On the other hand, there is no way by which he can be relieved of the responsibility of decision in concrete situations. To give him precise instructions to be literally carried out is to rob him of his moral responsibility as a person. It is not the function of the clergy to tell the laity how to act in public affairs, but to confront them with the Christian demand and to encourage them to discover its application for themselves. Hence between purely general statements of the ethical demands of the Gospel and the decisions that have to be made in concrete situations there is need for what may be described as middle axioms. It is these that give relevance and point to the Christian ethic. They are an attempt to define the directions in which, in a particular state of society, Christian faith must express itself. They are not binding for all time, but are provisional definitions of the type of behaviour required of Christians at a given period and in given circumstances. How these middle axioms are arrived at is a question which we shall examine in the next chapter.

In the meantime it may help to make the issues clearer if we take note of certain questions raised by Professor Tawney in a paper written in preparation for the Conference. He states the opposition between the Christian understanding of life and the standards and values of modern society in the following terms: "Its emphasis on the supreme importance of material riches; its worship of power; its idealization, not merely of particular property rights, but of property in general and as an absolute; its subordination of human beings to the exigencies, or supposed exigencies, of an economic system; its erection of divisions within the human family based, not on differences of personal quality or social function, but on differences of income and economic circumstance—these qualities are closely related to the ends which capitalist societies hold to be all-important. In such societies, as the practice of the latter clearly shows, they are commonly regarded, not as vices, but as virtues. To the Christian they are vices more ruinous to the soul than most of the conventional forms of immorality."

The conflict between the prevailing practices of society and the Christian attitude to life becomes especially acute in regard to the principle of equality. This principle does not mean either that all men are equal in capacity or that they all ought to fulfil the same functions, or that they all have identical needs. What it does mean is that all men, merely because they are men, are of equal value, and that such differences as will still exist in a juster social order must be made "not on the externals of class, income, sex, colour, or nationality, but on the real needs of the different members of the human family. All social systems and philosophies which discriminate between men on the basis, not of individual differences, but of these externals, are anti-Christian." It is the duty of the Christian Churches to "assert that class privilege, and the gross inequalities of wealth on which it rests, are not only a hideously uncivilized business, but an odious outrage on the image of God. While recognizing that change must necessarily take time, they should state frankly that the only objective which can satisfy the Christian conscience is the removal of *all* adventitious advantages and disabilities which have their source in social institutions. They should throw their whole weight into the support of measures calculated to lead to that end."

A first step towards the achievement of equality so interpreted is to insist on its application in the sphere of the care and education of the young. It ought to be possible for civilized people, let alone Christians, Professor Tawney suggests, to insist that young people, up to, say eighteen, shall be treated as outside the social conflict and to refrain from ruining their lives by importing into them the vulgar irrelevancies of class and income. "Is it too much to ask that the spokesmen of Christian opinion should say publicly and constantly that our callous neglect of these young lives is an odious national crime? Is it unreasonable to suggest that they should throw their whole weight on the side of a policy designed to ensure that all children and young persons, from birth to eighteen, shall be secured, as far as social action can secure it, equal opportunities of making the best of the powers of body, mind, and character with which they have been endowed? . . . These are not matters with which the Churches can properly regard themselves as having no concern."

To these illustrations from Professor Tawney's paper we may add one other. It relates to the meaning and use of power. In one of the most decisive and revolutionary of His recorded sayings Jesus drew the sharpest distinction between the values of His own Kingdom and those prevailing in the world. "Ye know," He said, "that the rulers of the Gentiles lord it over them, and their great ones exercise authority over them. Not so shall it be among you." He illuminated in a flash the problem of power, which is central in the relations of men with one another, and which in spite of its importance has received less attention from Christian thought than it deserves.[1] The word power is highly ambiguous. Power in the sense of validity, adequacy, effectiveness is a quality of being, and the more persons possess it the more they can help their fellows. But power in the sense which concerns us here is power over other men. In that meaning also it may have its legitimate place in the relations of men with one another. It may be an authority derived from God, for the right exercise of which men are responsible to Him. But in the form of power over others it has in it a demonic quality tending always to its perversion. It would seem as though sinful human nature could not be trusted to use this power over other men without abusing it. Jesus asserts in the most emphatic terms that to belong to His Kingdom is to renounce such power;

---

[1] Cf., however, the paper by Professor Vycheslavzeff in *Die Kirche und das Staatsproblem in der Gegenwart*, and Tillich: *The Interpretation of History*, pp. 179–202.

or (we may perhaps infer), if in the discharge of their worldly responsibilities, His followers are called to exercise it, they must do so in a continual awareness of its dangers. No issue touches the life of men so closely to-day as that of power and its use. In the economic sphere it is the power of some men to control the lives of others, much more even than the inequalities of wealth, that is the fundamental cause of social bitterness and strife. In the political sphere, science has placed in the hands of those who control the modern state possibilities of power undreamed of by earlier generations. The full extent of what can be done by those who hold the reins of power is only beginning to be disclosed. Men to-day, as Mr. Bertrand Russell has put it, are in danger of becoming drunk with power. "The love of power has thrust aside all the other impulses that make the complete human life."[1] This clear insight by one who is not a Christian into the great struggle which is taking place to-day in the souls of men should rouse Christians from their apathy and help them to realize that in it all that the Church means and believes is at stake.

Each of these illustrations raises issues the adequate treatment of which would require a volume to itself. They have been introduced only to give point to the question whether acceptance of the Christian revelation of the meaning of life does not necessarily involve certain attitudes and forms of behaviour which are in sharp opposition to the habits of ordinary society, and whether we can expect the world to pay serious attention to Christian preaching unless Christians not only proclaim these principles but act on them. Action is something which other men cannot avoid taking into their calculations. Has Christianity anything distinctive to say about the way men ought to act towards their fellows? If it has,

[1] *The Scientific Outlook*, pp. 274, 156.

then the leaders of the Churches, Mr. Tawney urges, ought, "whatever the cost, to state fearlessly and in unmistakable terms what precisely they conceive that distinctive contribution to be. If they do not, then let them cease reiterating secondhand platitudes, which disgust sincere men, and bring Christianity into contempt."

3. POLITICAL ACTION

When we approach the question of the action proper to the Church in the political sphere we find on both sides of a disputed field a considerable area of agreement. It is widely agreed that it is the task of the Church to proclaim and interpret the ethical implications of the Gospel. The Christian ethic cannot be accepted and acted on without resulting consequences in the political field. In many situations Christians cannot act in accordance with the principles of their faith without provoking political controversy. In a memorandum submitted by a group of leading churchmen in Germany it is recognized that, while it is not the business of the Church to interfere in the policies of the State, it is none the less necessary for the Church, in virtue of its responsibility for the spiritual welfare of the nation, to judge whether these policies in their fundamental tendencies are likely to benefit or injure the soul of the people. In the latter case the Church must pronounce against them. That is, however, not political but pastoral action. No clear dividing-line can be drawn between the sphere of the Church and that of the modern cultural state. Where the controlling ideas and aims of the State are contrary to the Gospel, a collision between the Church and the State is unavoidable.

The ethical witness of the Church includes the prophetic denunciation of evil. As *ecclesia militans* it is at war with everything that is contrary to the purpose of God. It is committed to fighting the battles of the Lord, scaling "every crag-fortress that bids defiance to the true knowledge of God."[1] As was said in an earlier chapter,[2] if the Church is true to its commission, its message will be a disturbing message. To say peace, peace, when there is no peace,[3] is to betray its trust and to make itself a cipher in the life of the time.

Signor Mussolini in one of his speeches has expressed the view that the solution of the relations of Church and State lies in the recognition that the State is sovereign in the temporal sphere while the Church is acknowledged as sovereign in its own proper sphere of the salvation and cure of souls. Some of the leaders of the German state claim that the State has the right to control and direct the whole of man's earthly existence, while it may be left to the Church to care for his interests in another life. In England also churchmen have been told by politicians that the Church has nothing to do with politics. These doctrines recall, though with a different emphasis, the teachings of Gelasius. They might be accepted, if Christianity were concerned solely with another existence and the salvation of a man's soul had no consequences for conduct in this life. But if the Christian redemption means redemption to live as God's children in this world, there can be no escape from the tension between the claims of the State to order the whole of life and the demand of God for a total obedience to His will. The obedience of men to the will of God must have, as it has had throughout Christian history, immense and incalculable consequences in the social and political spheres. The Church, by the mere fact of its existence, is a political factor of cardinal importance.

[1] 2 Cor. x. 5. Arthur S. Way, *The Letters of St. Paul.*
[2] Page 174. [3] Jer. vi. 14; viii, 11.

Further, there is widespread agreement that, whatever limitations there may be on the action of the Church as an organized society, Christians must give expression to their faith not only in what one may call the pre-political sphere of the aims, standards, and values that determine political action but also in the field of concrete political decision and political struggle. To doubt this would be to deny the sovereignty of God over the whole of life and to surrender large areas of life to the unfettered control of the forces of evil. The inactivity of Christians in the political sphere would sap the vigour of Christian life since it would be denied the opportunity of outward expression. Whether Christianity counts for little or much in the years before us will depend less on the doctrinal beliefs which Christians profess, necessary as these are as the basis of conduct, than on the tenacity with which they hold to the spiritual values implied in these beliefs and the determination with which they seek to realize them in practice.

There can be no question, therefore, that the Church must bear its witness in the political sphere through the faithful and energetic performance by its members of that which as Christians they believe to be right. It is a quite different question how far the Church in its corporate capacity should intervene in political affairs. The confusion of these two wholly distinct questions has clouded discussions of the relation of the Church to political action and hampered the effective exercise of Christian influence on public affairs.

The difficulty about the intervention of the Church as an organized society in the sphere of politics arises from the fact that the Church is a society organized for other purposes than political action. If it enters the political arena it runs the risk of obscuring or compromising the purposes for which it exists. We have already insisted that these purposes may also be obscured and compromised if Christian faith fails to express itself in the political sphere. The difficulty lies, further, in the fact that action by the Church as an organized society means to a large extent action by those who hold office in the Church, i.e. by the clergy, or by assemblies in which the influence of the clergy is predominant. The question which calls for consideration is not whether the influence of the Church should be exerted in the political sphere—this, as we have seen, is unavoidable—but whether and to what extent the influence of the clergy should be exerted in that field.

Here again there is wide agreement up to a certain point. No one to-day desires that the Church, as an ecclesiastical organization, should assume the direction of political or economic life. It is an advance and not a retrogression, as the Master of Balliol has pointed out in his little book on *Christianity and Economics*, that in the modern world the political and economic spheres have emancipated themselves from the ecclesiastical control to which they were subject in the Middle Ages.[1] The subordination of political to religious organizations had results so undesirable as to excuse in some measure the extremist reactions of Macchiavelli and Hobbes.

Thus in theory (whatever may be the shortcomings in practice), there is no serious disagreement on the fact that, on the one hand, the Church in its preaching and teaching has to bear a clear and outspoken witness on ethical questions, and that, on the other hand, any form of clerical domination over political and economic life is wholly undesirable. But since there is no clear and sharp dividing line between the aims of political action and concrete political decisions, there remains open a large field of debate in regard to the right course to be followed

[1] Pages 10 ff.

in practice. Both because the questions which arise are infinitely various in character, and because the right course for a Christian individual or assembly to take in a particular instance cannot be determined in advance by any abstract rule, but must be an act of obedience to God in face of the concrete situation, we cannot do more here than direct attention to certain general considerations on both sides which must be kept in view in reaching a decision.

On the one hand, we need to be alive to the danger lest in undertaking action in the political field the Church should compromise its character as Church. In entering the political sphere it becomes committed to the pursuit of relative ends and involved in the compromises inseparable from political action. The Church is a worshipping community in whose worship every relative political judgment is brought to the searching test and scrutiny of an absolute and divine judgment. There is a danger of this being forgotten if the Church in its corporate capacity commits itself to a political programme. The transition from a religious to a political loyalty is easily made, and there may be a subtle and unobserved substitution of other interests and motives for those which it is the special concern of the Church to foster. Just in proportion as the Church becomes involved in the political arena there is a danger of a loss of religious depth. The attempt to commit the Church to social and political programmes may be a short cut by which we seek to escape from the more difficult and costly responsibility of submitting ourselves to those deeper changes of disposition and outlook which are in the end a much more powerful revolutionary force.

A second ground for caution is that in every political action there is involved not only a choice of ends but also of the means most appropriate for achieving them.

Decisions in regard to the means best adapted for the realization of chosen ends involve rational judgments regarding the appropriateness and efficacy of particular measures. On these matters there may be legitimate differences of opinion among Christians. The Church has no right to commit its members to a particular view of them. As Church it unites men in a loyalty which transcends the relativities of political action.

A third reason why ecclesiastical assemblies need to discriminate as clearly as possible between the ethical guidance which it is their responsibility to give to members of the Church (which, if it is not to be insipid and innocuous, must have reference to concrete evils), and a judgment on the measures by which these evils should be remedied, is that decisions in regard to the latter can be properly taken only by those who have responsibility for the decision. Seen from the inside a problem has many aspects that are concealed from an outside view. Only those who have to act can reach a responsible decision. Advice divorced from responsibility is dangerous. It is a healthy thing that the expert should be exposed to criticism. But it is not good for society that the judgment of the trained statesman or the experienced civil servant or the practical business man should be replaced by the opinions of well-meaning amateurs. What lay at the root of the ineffectiveness of the Church in the Middle Ages, as Dr. Lindsay points out, is that the condemnation of evil practices in economic and political life "came from people who lived outside the practical difficulties. One set of men, the clergy, were laying down rules for another set of men, instead of inspiring these men to lay down rules for themselves."[1]

On the other hand, it does not follow from the existence of these real dangers and the necessity of guarding

[1] *Christianity and Economics*, p. 144.

against them that the Church should refrain from throwing the weight of its influence on occasion on the side of particular efforts of social, humanitarian, and political reform. Life is full of dangers, and we may betray our cause by caution and inaction as well as by rashness and unwisdom. When it has become clear to the Christian mind that certain evils are intolerable and must be ended, this sentiment must find some means of expression. It might ideally be best that the Christian conscience should exert its influence through associations of Christians for the achievement of specific objects. Many such organizations exist, either on a definitely Christian basis or drawing their support largely from Christians. But where such associations are not in existence or are inadequate for the purpose in view, we have to ask, as practical men, whether there is any other method by which the Christian conscience can find collective expression, except by voicing its demands through the assemblies and courts of the Church. The history of the Churches in the United States and in Great Britain, to limit our discussion for the present to these two countries, shows many instances of effective intervention by the Churches on behalf of causes of moral and humanitarian reform. Christian opinion voiced by the assemblies and courts of the Church has had a definite influence in shaping public policy. It would be of great interest if a historian could write in detail the story of these efforts. The reproach against the Church is not that it has been too active in these matters, but that it has been far too acquiescent in social injustice, and that in consequence its Christian witness has been discredited and lost its sting. If action in political and social matters by synods and councils is condemned, what alternative method is there by which the Church may prove itself, not in word only but in deed, to be an effective force for righteousness? If the only choice is between serving the cause of God in imperfect, faulty, and all too human ways or withdrawing from the dust and heat of the conflict and allowing the forces of evil to go their way unchallenged and unchecked, the former would seem to correspond most nearly with the obligations of those who are called to be soldiers of Christ. When truth and falsehood, right and wrong, are in the balance, it may be "less pardonable to be silent than to say too much."[1]

Again, just because the border-line between ends and means cannot be easily drawn, it may be legitimate and desirable for the Church, when it has reached a clear conviction that particular social evils must be remedied, to form its own judgment in the light of expert knowledge how this may best be done, and to submit these conclusions to the public judgment. Sir Josiah Stamp is of opinion that the Church may quite well have its own experts in these matters. While holding that the real task of the pulpit is not with the technique of the political and economic machine at all, he would "welcome occasional instances of men with a real aptitude for it undergoing the necessary discipline and study, fully equal in time and attention to that which they would have to give to any other expert or professional curriculum."[2]

What seems to be clear is that when the Church desires to say how effect should be given in practice to its ethical demands, before expressing a judgment it should undertake a thorough examination of all the factors in the situation. The present writer once expressed to the head of an important government department in a country which shall be nameless, lest there should appear to be any reflection on a particular group of Churches, his appreciation of the generous and unreserved help the administrator was

[1] Tawney, *The Rise of Capitalism*, p. 287.
[2] *Method and Motive in a Christian Order*, p. 196.

giving to a particular inquiry under the auspices of the Church; to which the head of the department replied that it had seemed to him so unusual to find a Church organization that wanted to ascertain the facts before passing a resolution on the subject that he felt that the undertaking deserved every encouragement. The gibe was not meant to be taken too seriously. The instance in question is not an isolated one. The Federal Council of the Churches of Christ in America has had for nearly twenty years a Department of Research and Education which has produced a number of valuable objective reports on social questions. But no one conversant with the practice of Church and religious bodies can question that the administrator's remark was not wholly wide of the mark. It should be a principle, to the application of which there ought to be no exceptions, that the Church as an organized society should not pronounce on questions of political policy or industrial practice until it has not only ascertained all the relevant facts, but also submitted these facts and the conclusions drawn from them to those who have to deal in a practical capacity with the questions involved.

A guiding principle for the relation between ends and means is given happy expression in a letter from a correspondent with a wide experience of public life in England. The material framework of life, says the writer, i.e. the way people get their incomes and spend them, affects the whole of individual existence. It calls certain motives into play and blunts others. The Church cannot therefore be indifferent to the structure of this material framework of life. It must test economic institutions by the ways in which they affect what it believes to be the good life. But what the Church has to insist on primarily is that that test be applied. It must recognize that in applying it differences of knowledge, understanding, insight, and sensitiveness may lead different people to different conclusions. If, for example, with reference to the rebuilding of Adelphi (a district in London near the Strand famous for its architecture by the brothers Adam in the eighteenth century) a Christian says, "I find Adelphi Terrace uninteresting and would prefer a handsome modern skyscraper," there is no reason why in spite of his taste he should not remain a member of the Church. But if he says, "I think Adelphi Terrace beautiful, interesting, and historic, but of course it must go, because naturally it will pay the owner of the site to rebuild," then (says the writer we are quoting) he ought to be excommunicated with bell, book, and candle.

4. RESOLUTIONS AND PRONOUNCEMENTS

A brief reference must be made to the passing of resolutions and the making of pronouncements by Church assemblies and other religious organizations. These may serve two important purposes.

The first is the spiritual and moral education of the members of the Church. It is a necessary and important function of the authorities of the Church to provide Christian people with ethical guidance. Not only is there no objection to pronouncements which have this end in view, but there is a definite obligation resting on the authorities of the Church to furnish such advice and help. Authoritative statements of this kind may often be a strength and support to individual ministers in interpreting the ethical implications of the Gospel in face of criticism and opposition.

The second purpose which pronouncements by Church assemblies may serve is to exert an influence on public opinion and through it on the policy of the State. This point has already been considered. Where there is a strong conviction among the membership of a Church on a particular issue it is natural and legitimate that this should be made known.

On the other hand, the practice of passing resolutions and making pronouncements is beset with dangers and may often be a sheer waste of time. Attention must be called to these dangers since the practice in question often diverts attention from methods of dealing with social and political questions that would be much more effective. Reliance on mistaken or futile methods of procedure cannot but weaken the influence of the Church for good.

Public pronouncements are honest only when they actually represent the opinions of those whose opinions they profess to represent. Dr. Ernest Johnson, who has had large experience in these matters, has called attention to the futility and dishonesty of committing a Church to expressions which "are no more than wishful thinking on the part of a minority."[1] Unreality of thought and statement ought to be avoided at all costs, if the testimony of the Church is to be effective. Pronouncements ought to be responsible pronouncements and it ought to be clear who are committed by them. It is surprising how often the sense of responsibility may be lacking in Christian assemblies. The danger is perhaps greatest in interdenominational and international bodies, in which sometimes resolutions are passed as an expression of the Christian mind on a particular public issue, when they do not in fact represent more than the opinions of the more or less chance collection of individuals who happen to be present at the meeting. Pronouncements which do not have behind them a solid body of considered and convinced opinion can have little or no effect on public action. Astute politicians and experienced civil servants are quite capable of assessing the amount of real force

[1] *The Church and Society,* p. 86.

which lies behind such resolutions and of attaching to them the weight that they deserve.

Secondly, the habit of passing resolutions carried to excess defeats its own purpose. Constant repetition dulls the effect. Where opinions are easily, cheaply, and glibly expressed, they are accorded little public attention. They may, if couched in sensational terms, attract a passing interest, but they have no deep or lasting effect.

Finally, we have to take account of the immense amount of valuable time, that might be expended much more fruitfully in other directions, which is often spent in the passing and debating of resolutions. The difficulty of discovering a form of words which neither says something wholly innocuous nor on the other hand becomes precise in matters in regard to which opinion differs, may lead to long hours of debate, resulting in the end in the adoption of a formula which is an evasion rather than a solution of the problem and which those who in fact disagree are able to accept because each is able to interpret it in his own sense. Christian assemblies must not allow themselves to become involved in futilities of this kind, if the influence of the Church is to count in a world in which there are movements that are in deadly earnest.

5. THE CHURCH AND HERESY

In considering the action of the Church in relation to questions of public policy and conduct an important distinction has to be made between occasions on which the Church lends its support to particular proposals for social or humanitarian reform which have the approval of a considerable body of its members and those occasions in which in a much more fundamental way the Christian faith is itself involved. In the former case it is a question whether a particular course of action is the best or wisest in given circumstances, and if mistakes are made no greater harm is done than by other manifestations of human fallibility. In the other case matters are more serious. A decision has to be made about the content and substance of the Christian faith. The Christian Churches at the present time are for the most part disinclined to exercise discipline in matters either of belief or of conduct, except in extreme cases or in the particular question of divorce. It may be, however, that conflict with the new pagan tendencies of our time may compel the Church at certain points to define what is, or is not, compatible with the Christian faith. We raise this question not to express a judgment on it but to call attention to its importance.

What is involved may be made clearer by a reference to the correspondence which took place a few years ago between Professor Gerhard Kittel and Professor Karl Barth. The former maintained in one of his letters that it was the privilege of the Christian to recognize everywhere the hand and finger of God. "If I stand by the side of Christ," he wrote, "I know nothing in the wide world—no sparrow on the roof-top, no lily in the field, no sacred history of Israel and the Jews 'under the law,' no history of Greek civilization 'without the law,' no Palestinian zealots and no Roman Emperor, no Mussolini and no Hitler—in which the Almighty Creator of heaven and earth, who has revealed Himself to me as the Father of Jesus Christ, does not exercise His sovereign sway." The name of Lenin was not included among the illustrations. Barth, in his reply, wrote, "Remain, if you think it right, under the swastika. It is equally possible to take one's stand under the Swiss cross, or under the double eagle, or under the Soviet star." Kittel, in a further letter, maintained that it is contrary to the nature of the Church to be unable to express a judgment on the concrete happenings of historical life. A Church that remained indifferent to what was taking place in the world, such as what happened on January 30, 1933, would deny the authority and responsibility entrusted to it by the Lord of the Church, who is at the same time the Lord of history. And he went on to assert in italics that "if the decision of world history in the life of a people lay between the Soviet star and the Germany of January 30th, the Church under God's Spirit and God's Word is not so poor as to lack full authority to say whether the decision of that day was from God or from Satan."[1]

If a Church declares a certain cause to be the work of Satan, it would seem to follow that it must exclude from its membership those who identify themselves with it. For, as St. Paul insisted, there can be no fellowship between Christ and Belial. The question therefore arises how far a Church is justified in expressing a judgment as a Church on historical events of this nature. Professor Karl Ludwig Schmidt, in commenting on this correspondence,[2] maintains that such judgments of historical happenings are not only permissible to Christians but are their definite responsibility and obligation; they cannot, however, be judgments of the Church. To admit the latter would be to recognize in the contingent events of history a second source of revelation independent of the supreme revelation of God in Christ. Moreover, a judgment of the Church must be judgment which is the judgment of the Church, for example, in France and in England, equally with the Church in Germany. A judgment of the Church is a judgment which declares that to hold the contrary view is to deny the Christian faith, and the Church through its authorities ought not to impose on its members as an article of faith a judgment into which there must enter an interpretation of the immense complexities of a historical situation.

---

[1] *Ein theologischer Briefwechsel*, pp. 10, 30, 34.
[2] *Theologische Blätter*, November 1934.

While many would agree with this judgment, the question remains whether there may not be attitudes and attachments in the political and economic spheres which the Church must declare to be irreconcilable with the Christian faith and consequently with membership of the Christian Church.

It is doubtful whether the Church can, or ought to, pronounce judgment on Communism, or Capitalism, or Fascism as such, since each of these comprises a bewildering variety of aims and activities, and the judgment becomes significant only when it is stated much more precisely what features in each are approved or condemned. A man may be a National-Socialist because he believes government by the party to be in the best interests of the nation, or a member of the Communist Party in certain countries because he regards its aims as leading most directly to the emancipation of the labouring classes, or a supporter of Capitalism out of a sincere conviction that under present conditions the sum of human misery would be increased and not diminished if any other system were substituted for it—and in all these cases still hold fast to his ultimate Christian belief. However vehemently other Christians may dispute any of these conclusions, and for themselves regard it as incompatible with the Christian understanding of life, it would be an unjustifiable and presumptuous confidence in the powers of human judgment to maintain that in our complex world only one reading of the facts of a highly intricate situation can be regarded as Christian.

This does not, however, preclude the possibility that within these wider complexes of facts issues may arise in regard to which the Christian Church must take a definite stand. The Church cannot avoid encountering in the world attitudes which are a plain denial of the Christian understanding of life, nor can it escape the necessity of dealing within its own borders with the problem of heresy. For example, the exaltation of the material above the spiritual in the activities of capitalistic society, the claim of the national state to be the ultimate authority in matters of faith and conduct, and the exercise of absolute power by dictatorships involving the destruction of human values are in complete opposition to the claims of Christian discipleship. The necessity may arise for the Church to denounce compromises with these anti-Christian forces as heresies which cannot be tolerated.

It may be that it is mainly by this negative path of rejecting certain beliefs and attitudes as irreconcilable with its faith that the Church will arrive at a clearer understanding of its mission and witness to modern society. If there is no specific Christian programme for social action, there are many forms of practice and action that are plainly incompatible with the Christian insight into the meaning of life. Just as in the early centuries the creeds of the Church took their shape largely through the repudiation of particular heresies as incompatible with the Christian faith, so in our time the path towards a clearer perception of the obligations of Christians in society may lie through the rejection of certain types of social conduct, social practice, or social organization as intolerable for the Christian conscience.

6. SOCIETIES AND ORDERS WITHIN THE CHURCH

It is probable that a large part of the pioneer work in this field will have to be undertaken not by the Church directly, but by societies and orders within it. The discovery of the points of fundamental conflict between the Christian faith and the forces which oppose it, and of the kind of witness and action that are demanded of

Christians, must be left, in the first instance, to groups within the Church who are willing to take risks and incur the danger of mistakes. New insights are limited in the beginning to the few, and the number of bold adventurers is never large. It is not right that the members of a minority should attempt to impose their views on the whole body, nor, on the other hand, that they should be hampered in their venture by the dead weight of an uninstructed and imperfectly Christian opinion and by the inertia and apathy of the mass.

To such groups of Christians committed to a definite way of life and to the accomplishment of a definite social purpose, Dr. Ernest Johnson applies the term sect, and he maintains that the incorporation of the sect in this sense within the wider and more inclusive body of the Church is "by far the most significant thing that can be said about the nature of the Church when we are seeking to discover its social function." Only thus "can the Church be kept alive and made to feel the most exacting demands of the Christian ideal upon the conscience in terms of social effort, and of that individual discipline which citizenship in the Kingdom requires. The small groups of adventurous and prophetic souls, bent on a radical attack upon society as it is, may thus maintain for themselves a fellowship of thought, feeling and action, and in so doing may gradually lift the entire membership to a higher spiritual temperature."[1]

7. THE CHURCH AS AN AGENCY OF RECONCILIATION

It is the task of the Church to contend with falsehood and error and to resist uncompromisingly what is contrary to its faith. But it is also its mission amid the confused struggles of political and economic life, in which

[1] *The Church and Society*, pp. 82, 216–17.

it is not easy through the mists always to distinguish friend from foe, to point to ends which lie beyond the relativities of temporal existence and to mitigate the bitterness of earthly struggles by uniting men in a fellowship which transcends these differences.

As Professor Reinhold Niebuhr has wisely written, "The fact is that, at its best, the sense of imperfection and the knowledge of forgiveness are the very basis of a vital social ethic. The worst human conflicts are conflicts between righteous men who are too self-righteous to know how evil they are. They are conflicts between nations and cultures who do not recognize how partial and relative is every value of human devotion. It is the human effort to make our partial values absolute which is always the final sin in human life; and it always results in the most bloody of human conflicts. Human conflicts are so terrible precisely because human beings are always engaged in the pretension of being like God, that is, fighting for some absolute and final good. A profound religion does not abolish all conflict in human history. But it mitigates every conflict by making men conscious of their creatureliness and finiteness."[1]

If it be true that it is possible, for reasons that have been stated, for a man to be a Communist and a Christian, or a Fascist and a Christian, then it would seem to be possible—to take the most extreme instance—that those who hold these conflicting allegiances should meet in the morning at the altar and later in the day at the barricades. This statement, made in an earlier draft of the paper, has been called in question by several correspondents. Those who reject the use of violence in all circumstances as unchristian cannot, of course, admit the second possibility. And it is certainly not for us to say

---

[1] *Doom and Dawn* ("World Problem Series," 347 Madison Avenue, New York).

what in any given circumstances is the right course for the individual to take.

Yet the conclusion to which the argument of the preceding chapters would seem to point is that Christians are meant to serve God with resolution and energy in political life—in an arena, that is to say, in which the use of coercion and force on occasion is unavoidable, and that, having made their choice, they have not to flinch, but to go through with it to the end. Their political loyalty may be an act of absolute devotion to the will of God, while they know at the same time that it is directed to a relative and temporal end. The paradox of Christianity is that it calls men to the whole-hearted service of God in the temporal sphere and at the same time deprives all earthly goods of ultimate value. This fundamental paradox of the Christian life finds expression in the words of Kierkegaard: "To abbreviate the hours of sleep by night, and to buy up every hour of the day, without sparing oneself, and then to understand that all this is jest—that is to be in deadly earnest."

The Church calls men into membership of a universal society transcending earthly oppositions and differences. In so doing it reminds men of their common humanity and of the truth that beyond the fierce conflict of ideologies and utopias is the reality of multitudes of ordinary, decent, kindly men and women with the same human interests and needs.

How the Church may both hold to this truth of its universality and at the same time by fearless, uncompromising action fulfil in each age its historical mission can be learned only by earnest seeking to know the will of God and courageous obedience to that will. At every moment and in every situation the Church has to face the responsibility of historical decision.

CHAPTER XI

THE SPRING OF CHRISTIAN ACTION

WE have considered the action of the Church in society, both in its corporate capacity and through the lives of its individual members. But we have not yet dealt with the fundamental question of the inspiration and guiding principles of Christian action. What are the factors that enter into and determine historical decision? How may the Church know and do the will of God?

In this concluding chapter limits of space do not permit of an attempt, such as was made in the chapter on the relation between the Church and the world, to present separately the different answers given by the various Christian traditions to this question. Nor perhaps would such a balancing of different opinions be generally desirable as the conclusion of the discussion. The most helpful contribution to the common task of oecumenical thought may be to try to state some of the major problems that seem to emerge from the line of thought that has been followed and to indicate some of the conclusions to which the argument seems to me to point. I shall try in doing this not to overlook other views and emphases. The one-sidedness and limitations which are inseparable from any individual presentation will receive the needed corrective in the discussions at, and following upon, the Oxford Conference. It is by the submission of tentative conclusions for criticism by other minds that thought is advanced and progress made towards a larger measure of agreement.

I. THE URGENCY OF THE PROBLEM

The question of the ends of life has become in our day more acute than ever. We live in a period of deep moral uncertainty. The question of the right life had not the same urgency for generations which lived in the shelter and security of a firm tradition. Western civilization has been built up on the basis of a conception of life derived from the Christian revelation and from the Hellenic and Roman traditions. With the rejection of the Christian foundations, it was only a question of time for the system of morals resting on these foundations to be called in question. We are living in the midst of an almost complete anarchy of ideas in regard to the principles which should govern both personal and social behaviour. The western world no longer possesses a unity. Rival conceptions of life, partly new and partly the revival of ancient beliefs, are struggling to impose themselves on society and to mould it in accordance with their own patterns of thought and behaviour.

In the midst of this conflict and chaos stands the Church, divided, perplexed, and relatively ineffective. The more clearly we see what needs to be done, the more deeply we are conscious of the present spiritual poverty. The sure insight, the fire, and the prophetic power for which the situation calls are lacking.

The call to the Church is to take its part in the creation of a new world. This high mission cannot be fulfilled merely by trying to revive or maintain traditional moral ideas, since moral ideas are always relative to historical situations, and the traditional moral values of Christianity are the expression of the response of the Church to the demands of a particular period. The task of a living Church is not to defend the forms inherited from a former age, but in loyal response to the call and guidance of

God in the present situation to create the new forms which that situation requires.[1]

2. AN ETHIC OF INSPIRATION

The only way by which the Church can accomplish the task to which it is called is by standing firmly on its own foundations. It must not allow itself to be brought into bondage to other forces. It must keep itself free from entangling alliances. It cannot, indeed, lift itself out of history, or dissociate itself from the life and thought of the age, nor can it do its work in the world without entering into combination with other movements that are reshaping human institutions. But it must jealously maintain the independence and purity of its own point of view. It must refuse to be brought into subjection to, or must emancipate itself from, nationalism, or capitalism, or humanistic liberalism, or any system of ideas not derived from its own central faith. Only from a centre beyond society can it criticize society and help it to reach a new orientation. We are brought back to the vital question with which our discussion began—whether human history has a decisive centre.[2] Without such a centre there is no criterion to give direction to historical action.

The basis of the Christian ethic is faith in a living, personal God who has disclosed His grace and His will in Jesus Christ. The gift and the promise are prior to any ethical demand.

From this general statement probably few Christians would dissent. But the truth on which we wish to insist, in opposition to much of the traditional interpretation

---

[1] Cf. an article by Dr. N. Stufkens in *The Student World* (Third Quarter, 1931).
[2] Pages 103 ff.

of Christian morality, is that the fundamental and characteristic thing in Christian action is not obedience to fixed norms or a moral code, but living response to a Person. We would reject decisively, with the Archbishop of York in his Gifford Lectures, the view which has long held the field in Christian thought and which conceives of revelation primarily as the communication of a deposit of truth, and agree with his insistence that "the knowledge of God can be fully given to man only in a person, never in a doctrine," and that "what is offered to man in any specific revelation is not truth concerning God but the living God Himself." God is at work in the world not as a static principle but as a living Person, "expressing His constancy through appropriate variations."[1]

What is distinctive in the Christian ethic is that it is what may be described as an ethic of inspiration rather than an ethic of ends. Its primary concern is with the source of action in a living fellowship with God, rather than with the goal to be attained. This view is at variance with the doctrine of a hierarchy of ends in the Thomist system—though that is not to say that the reality of personal fellowship with God which we desire to stress is not a living element in Roman Catholic piety. The view we are advancing differs also from many interpretations of the social gospel in which the emphasis is placed almost exclusively on the attainment of certain defined ends, and from any understanding of the Christian ethic which tends to put a new law in the place of the Gospel.

The view that the spring of Christian action is response to a God who is free and sovereign, who makes known His will in the living present to those who humbly seek to know it, does not involve any arbitrariness or individualism. The God to whom we are called to respond

[1] *Nature, Man and God*, pp. 299, 321–2.

is not capricious but constant in His dealings with men. In each new situation in which men find themselves His will can be learned only in the light of His will already revealed in Christ, in the Bible and in the experience of the Church. This will be brought out more fully in what follows. The truth which we desire to affirm finds its most adequate expression in the words of St. Paul, "Because ye are sons, God sent forth the spirit of His Son into our hearts"; and in his description of the new covenant, "not of the letter, but of the spirit; for the letter killeth but the spirit giveth life."

The primary concern of the Christian ethic is not with ends, purposes, or programmes, but with faith and obedience. The ends of life God has kept hidden in His own hands. God is Creator and calls men to be the agents of His creative activity. The contrast between the conception of God's activity implied in the Christian doctrine of God as Creator and any view achieved by Greek thought is strikingly brought out by Mr. M. B. Foster in his small volume on *The Political Philosophy of Plato and Hegel*.[1] The activity of the demiurge, as that of the craftsman, is conceived as the imposing of a given form on a given matter. But the Creator is free, not only from the latter of these limitations, but from *both*. This may be illustrated from the highest forms of art. The artist is not controlled by a preconceived plan. He has not an idea of his poem or picture which exists independently of the realization. God as Creator has not a purpose by which His activity is determined. Christians are called to share in His creative work, but this does not mean that they have a plan or programme, clear in its lineaments, for the realization of which they must work. Their calling is rather to observe how God is at work, to seek humbly to know His will and to obey His behests.

[1] Pages 180 ff.

> Here, work enough to watch
> The Master work, and catch
> Hints of the proper craft, tricks of the tool's true play.

Christ gave expression to this profound truth when He said "The Son can do nothing of himself, but what he seeth the Father do."

If action is to be effective in the social sphere it is, of course, essential that there should be definite objects of attack and pursuit. Without specific programmes nothing will be done. It is not for one moment suggested that the response of the Church to God's call should not issue in the adoption by the Church, or by groups within the Church, of particular policies for the redress of social evils. It has been already urged[1] that the formulation of middle axioms, defining the forms in which at a given period and in given circumstances the Christian law of love can find most appropriate expression, is an urgent need at the present time. Such collective judgments of the requirements of Christian conduct are not only permissible but imperative.

It is entirely consonant with the view that has been stated that the Church should recognize certain evils as those against which in our time it is specially called to contend, such as the exaltation of the material over the spiritual and the indifference to material injustice in capitalist societies, the demonry of nationalism, and the destruction of human values by dictatorships. We have already urged,[2] moreover, that it is necessary that Christians, individually and in association, should participate actively in movements for the establishment of social justice and the advancement of the common good. Only in this way can Christian faith become effective in the world of actual fact and prove that it has a meaning for the life that now is, as well as for that which is to come.

[1] Page 205.   [2] Pages 189, 214, 229.

The Christian ethic, in proportion as it is true to its own nature, is characterized, on the one hand, by a sober realism and restraining sense of human finitude, and, on the other hand, by a firm assurance of the ultimate triumph of the good. The Christian cannot surrender himself to utopian dreams of a Christian state, a Christian economic order, or a Christian world order. He knows that only Christian men can constitute a Christian society. He is under no illusions in regard to the reality and extent of the evil in the world. He is not a pessimist but a realist. So long as evil persists in men's hearts it will find in every new arrangement of society new forms in which to manifest itself. "Life," as Troeltsch maintained in a passage often quoted, "remains a battle which is continually renewed upon ever new fronts. For every threatening abyss which is closed, another yawning gulf appears."[1] The Christian attitude is opposed to any form of titanism. The responsibility for the world does not rest on human shoulders. It is in the hands of a higher wisdom. It is a foolish conceit that puny man is meant to carry the load of the universe.

But the Christian knows also that God is at work in the world and at war with evil. He knows that he is called to fight the Lord's battles. It is in the actual present world that he is called to serve God. It is there that he must encounter and attack the forces of evil. His concern therefore is to discover what are the specific tasks which in his time the Church is called by God to undertake. To these he will commit himself with his whole energy. He is distrustful of all ambitious programmes. He believes that God is the Lord of history and that history has a meaning. Vast issues may depend on men's fidelity and their response to the call of God; consequently, it is of great moment that the Church should be able to discern

[1] *The Social Teaching of the Christian Churches*, Vol. II, p. 1013.

the signs of the time and in each crisis of history fulfil its appointed task. But the results of human effort cannot be predicted, and the Christian is content to leave them in the hands of God.

In contrast with the Christian attitude, which is primarily concerned with the source and spring of action, the dominant faiths of the modern world—those of Liberalism and humanitarianism, of Communism, of National Socialism and Fascism—have this in common, that they all have in view specific goals which they hope to see realized within the temporal order. They are secularized forms of the Christian expectation of the Kingdom of God. They all reject the centre which for Christians gives history its meaning. Having abandoned the Christian hope, they either regard the Church as superfluous, or try to incorporate it as part of the social and political movement and make it an instrument for furthering their ends, or persecute it as a hindrance to the realization of their purposes. Yet in all these movements there are elements of truth. They are inspired by men's passionate desire for a new and better world. The ears of Christians ought to be open to the needs which these movements are seeking to meet, and to the hopes which they inspire. The Church is partly responsible for their emergence in history, since its preaching has too often tended to lay the whole emphasis on the salvation of the individual in a world beyond the present, and failed to proclaim a universal hope for the world.

It is not of course suggested that the Church should have its own political programme distinct from these other movements. It is both the strength and the weakness of Christianity that it has no specific political programme. The only practical choice to-day is between the systems that have been mentioned. If Christians are to take their share in the political life of the time, they have no alternative except to fulfil their political responsibilities within one or other of these movements. Having made their choice they are under obligation to give loyal support to the cause they have espoused. Yet it is always with a reserve. The Christian has to show a devotion equal to that of any, and yet never to forget that the end he is pursuing is a relative one. Within these movements Christians have their part to play as those who work loyally for the cause, and yet are continually bringing to bear on its aims and activities a criticism derived from their own perspective. They may thus help to redeem the movement of which they are a part from some of the dangers and weaknesses which are inherent in all human undertakings.

3. THE PROBLEM OF COMPROMISE

Action in the social and political spheres, whether by the Church or by individual Christians, involves co-operation with those who are not Christians. This brings up the question of compromise and the many perplexities which it creates for the Christian conscience. This is too large a subject for discussion here and the question of Christian obligation in the various spheres of the common life is the subject of other volumes in connection with the Oxford Conference. A brief reference may be made, however, to the bearing on the problem of the view of the Christian ethic which we have been considering.

It is important to be clear what the question is which primarily concerns the Christian. It is not in the first instance the question of the Christian solution of a particular problem of society. Given the assumptions on which society is attempting to deal with the problem there may be no specifically Christian solution. The primary question for the Christian is not how an un-

Christian, or partially Christian society may solve its problems, but how the Church, or the individual Christian, or a group of Christians, may in a given situation know and do the will of God. What must always be dominant in the mind of the Christian is the sense of his special vocation as a Christian, called to be God's instrument for the advancement of His Kingdom. We have already seen[1] how profound an influence, though often scarcely perceptible in its operation, may be exercised by those who thus bring into the activities of the common life a new perspective and new standards and values.

But the common purposes of society, in which the Christian participates, are never wholly identical with, and may sometimes be wholly contrary to, the ends which the Christian is called to serve. Has the dynamic view of Christian obligation which we have been considering any light to shed on the problem with which the Christian is confronted when those with whom he acts, and cannot help acting, do not share the Christian purpose?

The fact must always be faced that our natural indolence and cowardice continually tempt us to follow the line of least resistance and to compromise with evil. Experience shows only too plainly the extent to which Christians tend to conform to the prevailing standards of society. Every such compromise is sin, and has to be faced as such by each Christian in countless acts of daily decision in which his loyalty and fidelity are tested.

It is, however, another matter to allow ourselves to become perplexed and discouraged through a mistaken view of God's will as something static. The will of God, which we have to fulfil, is not an immutable law, existing in cold remoteness above the scene of the struggle, but the holy and loving will of One who understands and sympathizes with us in the conflict. While God's holiness

[1] Pages 202 ff.

calls us to be perfect as our Father in heaven is perfect, His will for us is not concerned with what might be done in an ideal world, but with what He desires in the present situation. We are not responding to Him as a Person when we detach the law of love from His living will in the present and set it up as an abstract ideal. There is a particular action which God wills that we should take in particular given circumstances, which in their totality we reverently accept as His ordering of the world. Our task is to discern that will and fulfil it.

This truth is dangerous for those with unlit lamps and ungirt loins. It may lead to a facile acquiescence in conventional standards as the best that is possible in the circumstances. But this is possible only if we forget the Cross, with its continual rebuke and challenge to our selfishness and complacency. It is the Gospel that is our great protection against surrender to the line of least resistance. If we think of Christianity primarily as demand, we tend to reduce the demand to what is within our compass. But if the Gospel is gift and promise, the love of Christ constrains us, and we are driven to press on to apprehend that for which we have been apprehended by Christ Jesus.

4. KURIOS CHRISTOS

The controlling factor in Christian decision is the truth expressed in the earliest of Christian confessions: Christ is Lord. Christian faith, we cannot remind ourselves too often, is the grateful and glad acknowledgment of a reality. Only if it has an objective and unalterable centre has it power to move the world. It finds its simple but adequate expression in the confession "Christ is Lord." This is the source, centre and end of Christian action; the ultimate touchstone of what is Christian and what is not Christian. All knowledge derived from other sources, however valid within its own range, has to be viewed in the light of this unique revelation and held in subordination to its supreme claims.

The Christian faith is faith in the Incarnation, the Cross, and the Resurrection. The Church in some of its branches and at some periods in its history has been tempted to lay the chief emphasis on one of these truths to the neglect of the others. Our need to-day is to recover the Christian faith in its wholeness.

We cannot make these assertions without reminding ourselves again[1] that for multitudes of men to-day they seem to have no relevance to the actual problems of life and to lack the vital meaning which would "command a total act of the whole moral being" and challenge men to a real decision. If we dare to make the confession *Kurios Christos* it must be with a deep awareness of the tasks to which it calls us.

Christ is no longer present in the flesh. How may the generation living to-day know of Him and believe in Him unless in some measure He is revealed in the lives of those who confess His name and in social institutions which are being transformed by His Spirit? It is this question which gives such profound significance to the Christian witness in social and political life.

What has enabled Christianity to survive is that in generation after generation it has found embodiment in lives of persuasive quality. Doctrine is often puzzling, but life is convincing. Conquest of fear, victory over circumstances, happiness springing from a fundamental faith in life, endurance, justice, mercy, compassion, and love are qualities which fill with a living meaning the word which is preached. To many minds Christian affirmations about the meaning of life are unconvincing because these have found too little embodiment in the actual

[1] Cf. pages 105 ff.

relations of men with one another in society. Too wide
a gulf between doctrine and life, subconsciously felt even
more than explicitly recognized in consciousness, has
invested the Christian scheme of life with a character of
unreality. The tremendous affirmations of the Christian
faith would seem more credible if the demand for the
acceptance of the truth of facts relating to the distant
past and of dogmas which for many are difficult to understand were re-enforced by the evidence of a society of
which these truths were the sustaining principle and
transforming power.

Faith in the Incarnation gives to human life a dignity
and value that are proof against all attacks of pessimism.

To believe in the Cross is to believe that God's love
is inexhaustible and that all His dealings with men are
prompted by His love. Those whose eyes have been
opened to this revelation are constrained in all their
relations with other persons to have the mind of Christ.
In the Cross, in which the life of Christ found its most
complete expression, lies the determining principle of
Christian action. "Unless there is in the Christian dis-
ciple," writes Professor H. H. Farmer,[1] "in the sphere
of human relationships an increasing sensitivity, practically implemented, to the infinite demands of the love
of God, to the shocking sin and tragedy of lovelessness,
to the costly way, revealed in Calvary, which must be
trod by God, and in some measure by those who know
God in Christ, if the thing is ever to be set right, it is
difficult to see what the specifically Christian vocation in
human life really amounts to in the end."

Faith in the Resurrection is the spring of undying hope.
Without the Resurrection the Cross is unrelieved tragedy.

[1] In a paper contributed to the forthcoming volume on *Christian
Faith and the Common Life*, in which this theme is impressively
developed.

The faith that Christ is risen is the assurance of the ultimate triumph of the good. We fall too easily into making
a "theology of the Cross" an excuse for our lack of faith
and powerlessness. The Church has no greater need than
a reborn faith that God has not abdicated and that Christ
is alive and carrying forward His work—a faith that will
free us from our timidity and inaction and send us forth
as fearless witnesses of the truth that the meaning of
human existence is revealed in Jesus Christ.

5. THE VENTURE OF FAITH

The assertion that the spring of Christian action is response
to the call of the living God needs to be guarded against
misunderstanding. There are those who conceive of the
individual as standing in stark isolation in the presence
of God listening to His command in the here and now
and acting in obedience to it. Any attempt to seek shelter
and refuge in a general principle or universal of any kind,
they would maintain, would be an evasion of the responsibility of concrete decision. But the truth is that every
concrete situation is shot through with laws, connections,
meanings. The individual takes into it his own past
experience, the influences of the tradition in which he
has been brought up and a conscience moulded by the
ideas and standards of the society to which he belongs.
He brings to his decision what he already is—his
previous experiences, the lessons of faith he has already
learned, the limitations which are the result of past slack-
ness and failure; an insight deepened, and a conscience
made sensitive, by the steeping of the mind in the profound truths of the Bible, or, on the other hand, a mind
incapable, by nature or training or past neglect, of
perceiving what God could reveal to one more sensitive
to spiritual things. God is not bound by a man's past,

but neither does He act in disregard of it. A right decision is not the outcome of the moment when it is made but is the fruit of many preceding acts of faith and obedience. The law of the spiritual life is that to him that hath shall be given, and a disciplined life is the condition of apprehending God's best and highest purpose.

The Christian, whether he is fully aware of it or not, makes his decisions as a member of the Church. In making up his mind what conduct is required of him as a Christian the individual is guided by the tradition of the Christian community of which he is a member. He draws on the rich heritage of Christian experience through the centuries. He models his conduct on the lives of other Christians he has known. Christian decisions are those which are made in obedience to the Word which the Church proclaims. They are the expression of lives nourished by the common worship and sacraments of the Church and educated and enriched through fellowship with other Christians. There is an element of immediacy and originality in all true Christian discipleship. But this is always combined with dependence on the wider experience and deeper insights of the Christian society.

Moments of creative and heroic choice may come to every man, when an unexpected emergency evokes all the latent resources of his nature and calls him to stake his life on his decision. But the majority of men ordinarily follow the beaten path. They are dependent on the guidance of pastors and teachers. They have to draw on the wisdom and insight of others. They need the leadership of prophetic spirits. The constitution of the Church is designed to meet these needs. God has given "some to be apostles; and some prophets; and some evangelists; and some, pastors, and teachers . . . unto the building up of the body of Christ."

In making his decision the Christian does not, and cannot, detach himself from the social tradition of the general community. The outlook of the individual has been formed by the ways of behaviour and scale of values prevailing in society. The tradition of the community sets its indelible impress on each individual and determines in large measure what he understands by good and evil. The current social practice is the soil out of which individual decisions grow. There may be acute conflicts between the Christian demand and the prevailing practice, but there are no sharp boundaries between the Christian ethos and that of the community. They act and react on one another. The Christian faith creates its own morality, but the raw material is provided by the prevailing custom. Inherited custom is given a new content and meaning when it is subordinated to the claim of God. It is no longer the same as it was before being christianized. Christian decision cannot avoid taking account of traditional moral standards because it is from these that ordinary men draw support and by these that their character is formed. The Christian task is not to destroy the traditions of the community but to purify and elevate them.

In Christian decision there is involved, further, an understanding of the situation to which the action relates. If we are to change reality we must first of all know it. The Christian who has to act in practical and public life has to act in the light of the best scientific knowledge available. This knowledge he obtains not from the Christian revelation but from rational processes. The experts on whose advice he relies may be Christians or non-Christians. In this field it is not piety but scientific excellence that is wanted. But there is never a sharp dividing line. The conclusions derived from scientific study may take on a new and deeper meaning when incorporated in the total Christian view of a situation and seen in its light.

All these factors enter into Christian decision, whether it is that of the Church or of the individual Christian or of a group of Christians. Yet when due weight has been given to each, the actual decision is a venture of faith. It is a living response in a new situation to the call of a personal God. To respond to an unconditional demand is always to reach beyond the security of experience and to put life to the hazard, to engage in a wager in which the stake is ourselves. Life cannot be lived, as great Christian thinkers like Pascal and Kierkegaard have insisted, without taking risks. A Church which would fulfil its mission in the world to-day must be one which is prepared to take large risks, or to allow its members to take large risks.

A right decision cannot be made in advance by a careful balancing of principles and considerations. It can be made only in the moment of decision itself. This does not mean that it may not and ought not to be preceded by a long period of reflection in which all the relevant factors are weighed and tested. Nor does it mean that there are not settled convictions and tried teachings of experience which for a good man are not open to question and which he would not dream of discarding. These are indeed the basis and condition of a right decision. The more important a decision the more necessary it is that a man should bring to it his total experience. But each situation is new and calls for a venture into the unknown. And for the Christian that venture is a response to what he believes to be the will of God.

It belongs to the nature of venturous decision that it may be mistaken. The Christian has indeed a light by which he can act. History has for him a centre which gives it a meaning. Christ has shown us what love demands.

We know in some measure the kind of life to which we are called. We can recognize that some things are wholly contrary to God's will. But this does not provide infallible guidance for concrete action or eliminate the responsibility and risks of decision. The Christian statesman may have misread the factors in a situation and may take a decision the consequences of which bring misery to millions. It is conceivable that a body of pacifists, acting from the sincerest motives, may by weakening resistance to aggression allow the establishment of tyranny for generations. In a world that is as yet far from Christian, that is in many of its manifestations definitely hostile to Christ, in a world so complex that the effects of action are unforeseeable and incalculable, we cannot say with confidence what forms of action will make a better order. Actions inspired by the noblest intentions may be caught in the vortex of human activity and struggle and produce results wholly different from those their authors willed. We can only act in faith and leave the results in the hands of God.

Since responsibility is real, and the consequences of decision unforeseeable, life would be impossible without the reality of God's forgiveness. It is because the Christian believes in atonement and in God's power to overrule our blunders and follies and sins and make them subserve His own unchanging purpose of good that he can act with confidence and courage, and decide without fear and without regret.

Christian action is staking everything on the reality of God, as He has been revealed in Jesus Christ.

6. DIRECTIONS OF ADVANCE

If there is to be a release of the creative energies which are brought to birth when men commit themselves in acts of faith and obedience to the will of the living God, what practical form may the fresh venture be expected to take? The course of our thought suggests two directions in which it may find expression.

The first is in the spontaneous activities of groups of many kinds which recognize and respond to the call to devote themselves to some particular task. No large response from the Church as a whole can be related to any single centre. The hours of the day are too few and human capacities too limited to permit of the organization from one centre of the infinitely varied responses which are demanded from the Church. It is given, moreover, only to an infinitesimal number of persons possessed of rare capacities and placed in positions of large public responsibility to exert more than a negligible influence on the concerns of society as a whole. What is in some measure in the control of each of us is our immediate environment. It is there that the Christian witness has to be borne and that Christian action can be taken. If the Church is to be a living force in the world its influence will be exerted through an endless multiplicity of "cells," consisting of persons who respond to a call to devote themselves to specific tasks in a limited environment. The separate and independent activities of such groups, drawn together for a great variety of different purposes, is one way in which a rebirth of Christian faith and love and of the creative energies which flow from them would find natural expression.

The other direction in which advance may be looked for has relation to the life of the Church as a whole. We have already been reminded[1] that while Christians differ deeply about the nature of the Church they all believe that there is, and can be, only one universal society acknowledging Jesus Christ as Lord. Yet to-day the

[1] Page 89.

Church is divided, not only in organization and government, but in the understanding of the Gospel and of its implications for conduct. The Church cannot hope in such a condition to meet the demands of the present situation. It is a vital question how advance may be made towards a larger unity.

Already the Churches are beginning increasingly to recognize their responsibility for one another. The concern or weakness of one is seen with growing clearness to be the concern of all. This consciousness of the universality and unity of the Church needs to be fostered by all possible means, and on the authorities of the individual Churches rests the responsibility for the systematic education of their members in an understanding of the nature of the Church as a universal society. It would seem natural also that the increasing appreciation of the oecumenical character of the Church and the deepening fellowship should seek expression in common action. Action, however, is always related to concrete situations, and the situations in different countries differ widely from one another. It is the Churches themselves that possess the necessary authority to act, and it is with them therefore that the responsibility for action lies. The extent to which such action can advantageously be fostered and co-ordinated by an international organization experience alone can show.

The field in which oecumenical co-operation seems to be most urgently needed and likely to be most fruitful is that of common study and thought. But by thought we do not mean thought divorced from action, but thought arising out of and directed towards the living conflicts and tasks of our time. This is not the type of thought which may be criticized as scholastic, academic, and lifeless, since it "does not arise primarily from the concrete problems of life nor from trial and error, nor from experiences in mastering nature and society, but rather much more from its own need of systematization."[1] What is required is the kind of thinking which will help the Church to see more plainly, amid the confused struggles of to-day, its proper tasks, to determine more clearly its relation to the forces that are shaping the modern world, and to know more surely the heresies which it must oppose if it would be true to its own faith. Such thinking would be related directly to action, since its aim would be to place at the disposal of those in the various Churches who have to take responsible decisions a growing body of knowledge to the shaping of which the ablest Christian minds in all countries and the insight and experience of the various Christian traditions would have contributed.

The task is one which can with the greatest advantage and greatest economy be undertaken by the Churches in co-operation on an oecumenical basis; with the greatest advantage, because it is the mind of the universal Church with its variety of historical experience and its wealth of different traditions that must be brought to bear on the problem; and with the greatest economy, since the necessary resources will be hard to find, both in money and, still more, in personnel, inasmuch as the persons possessing the combination of qualities and the training necessary for guiding such an undertaking are at present few.

The problem which confronts those who are unable to submit themselves to the rule of a single, central, ecclesiastical authority is how, without surrender of the priceless gift of freedom, they may escape the danger of splitting the truth into fragments and may remain bound together in a common loyalty to a common faith. The only alternative to truth imposed by authority is truth freely accepted because of its inherent power and per-

[1] Mannheim, *Ideology and Utopia*, p. 10.

suasiveness. Is it possible for those who, in spite of their real and deep differences, are yet in agreement about what gives to human history its central meaning, and who are united in the common confession, "Christ is Lord," to make provision for thinking out together the implications of this faith and its significance for the social and political tasks of our time? May we hope that, if it were possible to enlist the help of the best Christian minds and the deepest Christian insight on which the universal Church can call, there might progressively come into being a body of Christian thought which, hammered out under the criticism of many different minds, and richly fed by the various streams of Christian experience and tradition, might possess a comprehensiveness, balance, and depth that would win for it increasingly wide acceptance freely rendered, and draw together in a deepening mutual understanding those who are now separated? Progress would thus be made towards Christian unity along the surest lines, since it would be by the path of free, inward, spiritual agreement. That would seem to be the great adventure to which the Church in this time may be called.

The Church is not far from the end of the second millennium of its existence. Empires rise and fall and movements take their rise and spend their force. The Church can afford, and ought, to take long views. It has not only to think of the responsibilities of to-day and of to-morrow but to prepare for what the unknown future may bring. In the midst of what seem to be great events weak men, who yet know in whom they have believed, are called to play their part in history. If by a power which is not our own we are enabled to make the ventures to which God may be calling us, it will be in the strength of the assurance given to us in the words, "Ye have not chosen me, but I have chosen you."

INDEX OF NAMES

INDEX OF SUBJECTS

GEORGE ALLEN & UNWIN LTD
LONDON: 40 MUSEUM STREET, W.C.1
LEIPZIG: (F. VOLCKMAR) HOSPITALSTR. 10
CAPE TOWN: 73 ST. GEORGE'S STREET
TORONTO: 91 WELLINGTON STREET, WEST
BOMBAY: 15 GRAHAM ROAD, BALLARD ESTATE
WELLINGTON, N.Z.: 8 KINGS CRESCENT, LOWER HUTT
SYDNEY, N.S.W.: AUSTRALIA HOUSE, WYNYARD SQUARE